THE MODERN BRITISH HORROR FILM

QUICK TAKES: MOVIES AND POPULAR CULTURE

Quick Takes: Movies and Popular Culture is a series offering succinct overviews and high-quality writing on cutting-edge themes and issues in film studies. Authors offer both fresh perspectives on new areas of inquiry and original takes on established topics.

SERIES EDITORS

Gwendolyn Audrey Foster is Willa Cather Professor of English and she teaches film studies in the Department of English at the University of Nebraska, Lincoln.

Wheeler Winston Dixon is the James Ryan Endowed Professor of Film Studies and Professor of English at the University of Nebraska, Lincoln.

Steven Gerrard, *The Modern British Horror Film*
Daniel Herbert, *Film Remakes and Franchises*
Ian Olney, *Zombie Cinema*
Valérie K. Orlando, *New African Cinema*
Steven Shaviro, *Digital Music Videos*
David Sterritt, *Rock 'n' Roll Movies*
John Wills, *Disney Culture*

The Modern British Horror Film

STEVEN GERRARD

RUTGERS UNIVERSITY PRESS

New Brunswick, Camden, and Newark, New Jersey, and London

Library of Congress Cataloging-in-Publication Data
Names: Gerrard, Steven, 1970– author.
Title: The modern British horror film / Steven Gerrard.
Description: New Brunswick : Rutgers University Press, 2017. |
Series: Quick takes: movies and popular culture |
Includes bibliographical references and index.
Identifiers: LCCN 2017014956 (print) | LCCN 2017033132 (ebook) |
ISBN 9780813579450 (E-pub) | ISBN 9780813579467 (Web PDF) |
ISBN 9780813590059 (hardback) | ISBN 9780813579443 (paperback)
Subjects: LCSH: Horror films—Great Britain—History and
criticism. | BISAC: PERFORMING ARTS / Film & Video /
History & Criticism. | SOCIAL SCIENCE / Popular Culture. |
PERFORMING ARTS / Film & Video / Guides & Reviews. |
SOCIAL SCIENCE / Media Studies.
Classification: LCC PN1995.9.H6 (ebook) |
LCC PN1995.9.H6 G385 2017 (print) |
DDC 791.43/61640941—dc23

A British Cataloging-in-Publication record for this book is
available from the British Library.

∞ The paper used in this publication meets the requirements
of the American National Standard for Information Sciences—
Permanence of Paper for Printed Library Materials, ANSI
Z39.48-1992.

www.rutgersuniversitypress.org

Manufactured in the United States of America

THIS BOOK IS DEDICATED TO THE FOLLOWING:
PERRY, NAN, AND MY MUM FOR LETTING ME
WATCH LATE-NIGHT HORRORS; MY DAD FOR
LETTING ME WATCH *MATCH OF THE DAY* AND
GETTING ME TO SUPPORT BURNLEY FC AND THE
MIGHTY WALES; AND GRIFFTER, KLAUSE, AND
DOKTOR M, WITH WHOM I HAVE HAD ADVENTURES
GALORE, INCLUDING MAKING OUR OWN MODERN
BRITISH HORRORS WITH *THE NIGHT OF THE 26TH*
AND *SPACE VICAR—FROM SPACE*. THANK YOU ALL.

CONTENTS

THE MODERN BRITISH HORROR FILM

INTRODUCTION

Horror films are fascinating. They reveal the inner turmoil and angst that *we*, as a species, feel most frightened about. They make us shudder in fright, hide our eyes, or turn away from the screen. The best horror films also reveal something about the dark underbelly of humankind and the ways in which even the most kind, loving, and caring person can become a monster in every true sense of the word. The horror films that linger long in the memory remain those that have some sort of humanist element at their very core: Frankenstein's monster and the Wolfman remain desperately tragic; Count Dracula is always sexualized and predatory; and zombies, despite their often slow and shambling gait, remind the audience that belonging to a faceless and soulless society, where everything remains stagnant and decaying, is a logical outcome for all of us. It is this human element that makes the horror film so important to cinema, and its impact on reflecting the human condition cannot be underestimated.

As a species, we have vivid imaginations that allow us to see shapes in the fog, to be afraid of the unknown, and to fear all things improbable. Horror films provide their audience with a psychological need and desire to satisfy the cravings of this fear of the unknown. They are a chance for *us* to become, at least for a short while and from the comfort of our seats, the hero or heroine being chased by the monster or even the monster killing its victims. In keeping with the tropes associated with the Gothic genre, the horror film iconography includes decaying mansions, ruined castles, fog-shrouded landscapes, and dark and shadowed locales, while the human element covers a wide array of elements, including unknown supernatural forces, natural and man-made monsters, mad scientists, satanic villains, werewolves, vampires, ghosts, and of course, diaphanously clad victims.

The Gothic stories of Horace Walpole, Sheridan Le Fanu, Mary Shelley, Bram Stoker, Edgar Allan Poe, and others, the myths, folktales, and fables of eastern Europe, and the Grand Guignol of Victorian melodrama helped fan the flames of early horror cinema. The very first horror movie, *Le manoir du diable* (George Méliès, 1896) may have been only two minutes long, but it contained familiar horror elements such as a flying bat, the devil, skeletons, ghosts, a witch, her cauldron, and a haunted castle. Other early horror films often used literary sources, with notable examples including *Dr. Jekyll and Mr. Hyde* (Otis Turner, 1908), *Frankenstein* (J. Searle Dawley, 1910), and

Notre Dame de Paris (Albert Capellani, 1911). Japan's early foray into horror included *Shinin no Sosei*, aka *Resurrection of a Corpse* (director unknown, 1898), while Sweden produced *The Phantom Carriage* (Victor Sjostrom, 1921) and *Haxan: Witchcraft through the Ages* (Benjamin Christensen, 1922). The long-running French serials *Fantomas* (Louis Feuillade, 1913), *Les vampires* (Louis Feuillade, 1915), and *Judex* (Louis Feuillade, 1916) clearly demonstrated that horror films could use their literary cousins while remaining popular with audiences.

It was in Germany that *the* first bona fide horror cinema "movement" emerged. Films such as *Der Student von Prag* (Stellan Rye and Paul Wegener, 1913), *Der Golem* (Paul Wegener and Carl Boese, 1920), *Das Cabinet des Dr. Caligari* (Robert Wiene, 1920) and *Nosferatu* (F. W. Murnau, 1922) remain important films of the German Expressionist film movement. While the iconic image of the vampiric Nosferatu's shadow climbing a staircase will always be frightening, these films' reflection of the rise of fascism—as chronicled in Siegfried Kraceur's work *From Caligari to Hitler* (1947)—clearly defined how horror films could (in)directly begin to comment on the era in which they were made.

Much has been written on the horror genre, and each work has recognized the impact of German Expressionism on the genre. Carlos Clarens's *An Illustrated History of*

Horror and Science-Fiction Films (1967), Dennis Gifford's *A Pictorial History of Horror Movies* (1973), and Allan G. Frank's *Horror Movies* (1974) were excellent overviews that focused primarily on German Expressionist films, Universal Studios' *Frankenstein* and *Dracula* series, Val Lewton's chillers of the 1940s, Roger Corman's Poe adaptations, and the work of Hammer Films, Amicus, Tyburn, and Tigon. The excellent *The Encyclopedia of Horror Movies* (Hardy, 1986) provided both lavish illustrations and a chronological history of horror cinema's main films. From a British perspective, arguably the best of the overviews of British horror remains David Pirie's *A Heritage of Horror: The Gothic English Cinema 1946–1972* (1973), which firmly planted the British horror movement into both its Gothic and contemporary surroundings. Excellent modern overviews include Jonathan Rigby's *English Gothic: A Century of Horror Cinema* (2006), Barry Forshaw's *British Gothic Cinema* (2013), and Johnny Walker's *Contemporary British Horror Cinema: Industry, Genre and Society* (2016). Focusing purely on Hammer Films' large body of work, Dennis Meikle's *A History of Horrors: The Rise and Fall of the House of Hammer* (2009) remains an excellent and very welcome overview of "The Studio That Dripped Blood."

These latter books note that horror has moved away from its niche market into the sphere of more mainstream populist entertainment. The horror film spawned magazines such as *Famous Monsters of Filmland*, *Monster Mania*, *Monster Mag*, the *House of Hammer*, *Fangoria*, *Rue Morgue*, *We Belong Dead*, and *Dark Side*, which celebrate both old and new horror films with glee. Horror films are showcased at festivals like Fantasporto, FrightFest, and Fantastic Fest. The latest gorefests, ghost stories, or stalk 'n' slash films are screened to fans and "normal" audiences who either wish to celebrate *their* love and passion for all things horror or are curious as to what the fuss is all about. Many aficionados dress up as their favorite horror-film characters and not only attend the screenings but party long into the night dressed as ghosts, ghouls, and goblins of all descriptions. These festivals are also where the filmmakers gather to exhibit and celebrate the films they have made. As an example, Abertoir: The International Horror Festival of Wales has seen such horror luminaries as Luigi Cozzi, Lynn Lowry, Fabio Frizzi, Richard Johnson, Robin Hardy, and Doug Bradley talk about their work, while mingling with the crowds in the bar afterward. Likewise, academia has shown its interest in horror cinema. What was once deemed as nothing more than cult has now become normal, with conferences around the world celebrating, discussing, and analyzing horror across all media platforms. These developments clearly demonstrate that, despite the cyclical nature of genres, horror films may be around for at least the foreseeable future.

For the majority of horror fans, one name remains synonymous with British terror: Hammer Film Productions. From the 1950s through to the mid-1970s, Hammer, a small and independent production company housed in the comfy confines of its own studios just outside London, churned out Gothic horror movies with merry abandonment. It enjoyed global box-office success with its *Frankenstein* and *Dracula* series and created a horror legacy that made it, as David Pirie wrote, "the only staple cinematic myth which Britain can properly claim as its own, and which relates to it in the same way as the western relates to America" (9).

Hammer had hit on a willing formula. Using its own film studios at Bray meant that like Universal before it, its particular "house style" style was well in evidence by the mid-1960s. The studio's strong use of color; the recycling of sets, production designs, story lines, and themes (most notably the tropes of nineteenth-century Gothic literature); and the use of iconic actors like Peter Cushing and Christopher Lee meant that the company's name above the title, on the advertising billboards and posters at the cinema's doors, could only mean one thing: violence, sex, and horror (or at least what was permissible at the time).

Hammer was prolific. By using literary works in the public domain and therefore not having to pay any royalties, the company churned out Gothic horror after Gothic horror. Starting with *The Curse of Frankenstein* (Terence Fisher, 1957), it finished its franchise six movies later with *Frankenstein and the Monster from Hell* (Terence Fisher, 1973). The company's *Dracula* (or vampiric-themed) films ran to fourteen productions, while four *Mummy* movies saw the Egyptian undead trudging very slowly around cheaper and cheaper film sets. Hammer flirted with zombiedom through *Plague of the Zombies* (John Gilling, 1966), mythology with *The Gorgon* (Terence Fisher, 1964), and psychodramas like *Taste of Fear* (Seth Holt, 1961). But it was evident that the recycling of themes and styles would quickly tire for an audience wanting more vicarious thrills than Hammer dared offer.

The company's fortunes were not long-lived. While *Frankenstein Must Be Destroyed* (Terence Fisher, 1969) and *Hands of the Ripper* (Peter Sasdy, 1971) were interesting products of their time, Hammer did produce a lot of dross. For every epic like *One Million Years BC* (Don Chaffey, 1966), which saw a fur-bikini-clad Raquel Welch fighting off Ray Harryhausen's stop-motion pterodactyls, there was Martine Beswick's sultry tribe leader Queen Kari sitting astride a four-wheeled, plaster-of-Paris white rhinoceros in *Prehistoric Women* (Michael Carreras, 1967), which only added camp bemusement to the genre. It quickly became apparent that Hammer relied far too heavily on the Gothic template it had created. By the 1970s, it was both artistically and (virtually) financially bankrupt. Attempts at providing hip and trendy horrors such as *Dracula AD 1972* (Alan Gibson, 1972) were fun, campy, not frightening, and distinctly out of step with current attitudes long before the film's release.

Audiences' tastes had changed. Late-1960s American horror films were, despite their heritage link to Hammer, much more visceral. While Britain had the Swinging Sixties, America had the Vietnam War, civil rights movement, and Watergate to use as the backgrounds to its horror films. Films such as *Rosemary's Baby* (Roman Polanski, 1968), *The Night of the Living Dead* (George A. Romero, 1968), and *The Exorcist* (William Friedkin, 1971) were American, but it is not difficult to see that these are Hammer horrors in all but name. Even the lower-budgeted and exploitation areas, seen as tugging at the very heart of conservative America, were influenced by the company. Popular films like the Blaxploitation movies *Blacula* (William Crain, 1972) and *Blackenstein* (William A. Levey, 1973), the satanic-themed *Brotherhood of Satan* (Bernard McEveety, 1971), and the psychedelic *Werewolves on Wheels* (Michel Levesque, 1971) may have tackled popular themes of exploitation, but Hammer had done this conservatively for over a decade before. Britain's horror exploitation cinema was the same: Michael

Reeves's *Witchfinder General* (1968), James Kelly's *The Beast in the Cellar* (1971), and Pete Walker's *The Flesh and Blood Show* (1972) may seem at odds with each other in the horror canon, but they all have Hammer's influence well in evidence.

Hammer's influence was widespread. The French horror film *Eyes Without a Face* (Georges Franju, 1960) may not *look* or *feel* like a Hammer film, but it was certainly capturing the momentum of Hammer's releases. Jean Rollin's surrealist French vampires were highly eroticized French equivalents of Dracula's brides. Jess Franco's sexploitation horror and the Italian "giallo" work of Mario Bava and Dario Argento remain variations of Hammer's psychodramas. Spain's "Blind Dead" series owes more to *Plague of the Zombies* than to Romero's work. Hammer's influence on the world's horror stage was there to see.

But everything has its time. By 1976, Hammer's last bona fide horror production, *To the Devil a Daughter* (Peter Sykes), which had been filmed under strained conditions, was released to poor box-office returns. Despite attempts to keep the production company afloat through a move into television production, the company ceased trading in the 1980s. This was a shame, because British horror—as led by Hammer—was seen as influential on world horror and influenced new, up-and-coming American directors like George A. Romero, John Carpenter, and Tobe Hooper, as well as those with European sensibilities, like Georges Franju, Rollin, Bava, and Franco. These directors would have proved a godsend to 1970s British horror, and while British directors such as Pete Walker, Michael Reeves, and Norman J. Warren certainly kept the flag flying, they were in a losing battle.

Once vying for the marketplace alongside Hammer, its rival Amicus stopped production of their portmanteau movies. Films like *Doctor Terror's House of Horrors* (Freddie Francis, 1964), *Torture Garden* (Freddie Francis, 1967), *The House That Dripped Blood* (Peter Duffell, 1970), *Tales from the Crypt* (Freddie Francis, 1971), *Vault of Horror* (Roy Ward Baker, 1973), *From Beyond the Grave* (Kevin Connor, 1974), and *The Monster Club* (Roy Ward Baker, 1980) were interesting and had good casts and neat stories with stings in their tails. With the demise of Hammer, Amicus followed suit. Smaller production companies such as Tigon and Tyburn had tried to cash in on the horror boom, with a mix of "classic" Gothic tropes and modern-day horrors, but all to muted effect. Tigon finished film production in the early 1970s, moving into distribution and limping along through releases of dreadful soft-core porn films for the then-burgeoning VHS market. Tyburn Films may have used Hammer and Amicus personnel, but it remained strictly routine in its productions and fell into obscurity by the mid-1970s.

The demise of these companies was due in part to a collapsing British film industry. American investment stopped, talent moved to television or abroad, and audience tastes changed. There were some movies that boldly fought for the cause. There were three Dracula movies in 1979: *Nosferatu* (Werner Herzog) was a German remake, with Klaus Kinski in the central role; *Dracula* (John Badham) was a British/American coproduction that appeared to fair critical acclaim and box office ($20 million); but both movies were hampered by the release of the American comedy *Love at First Bite* (Stan Dragoti), which showed that the count was now only successful through parody. Keeping up the comedic elements was John Landis's *An American Werewolf in London* (1981), which had groundbreaking makeup effects and a tongue-in-cheek attitude toward its subject matter and was genuinely exciting, horrible, and ghoulishly fun. The cult horror writer Clive Barker was propelled from relative obscurity to cult director stardom with his modern spin on Pandora's box with the grim and graphic *Hellraiser* (1987). However, these stylish and influential efforts were few and far between.

With the American teen-slasher-flick series *Friday 13th* and *A Nightmare on Elm Street* taking center stage, it was no surprise that British horror was on the ropes. It seemed as if no one was prepared to make a horror film that strayed outside appealing to British audiences' sensibilities. Films like *The Company of Wolves* (Neil Jordan, 1984), *Paperhouse* (Bernard Rose, 1988), and *Dust Devil* (Richard Stanley, 1993) were far too artsy to appeal to most mainstream audiences, and they barely got a release. Others such as *Rawhead Rex* (George Pavlou, 1986), *Dream Demon* (Harley Cokeliss, 1988), *I Bought a Vampire Motorcycle* (Dirk Campbell, 1990), *Revenge of Billy the Kid* (Jim Groom, 1992), and *Funny Man* (Simon Sprackling, 1994) relied too heavily on British TV and genre stalwarts to capture an audience, which in turn emphasized their parochial approach to their subjects.

There were stronger entries with *Darklands* (Julian Richards, 1996) and *Razorblade Smile* (Jake West, 1998), and genre-hybrids like *Hardware* (Richard Stanley, 1990) and *Death Machine* (Stephen Norrington, 1994) demonstrated that there were the odd glimmers of hope for the British horror film, *provided* audiences could be found. But they couldn't. It was left to the overblown histrionics of megabudget coproductions of *Bram Stoker's Dracula* (Francis Ford Coppola, 1992) and its follow-up, *Mary Shelley's Frankenstein* (Kenneth Branagh, 1994), to remind British audiences that British horror (at least in name or just possibly *style*) was still alive.

In the 2000 article "Dying Light: An Obituary for the Great British Horror Movie," Richard Stanley argued that

British horror cinema had failed its potential to reach out to new audiences due to amateur efforts, poor distribution and exhibition, and talent that went elsewhere. The excellent work done by Jonathan Rigby of chronicling the British horror film ended on a rather sour note. He felt that the future of the genre was bleak and that the chances of a uniquely British approach to horror being reestablished were slim at best. However, this was all about to change.

It was assumed that the revival of the British horror film would look back to the past and the Gothic traditions of Hammer et al. To some degree, it did. But British cinema has always had a commitment to portraying realism. It was *this* approach that relaunched the genre to a new audience that used social media, new technologies, fan forums, and websites to seek out thrills. Going to the cinema is an expensive pastime. The advent of VHS, DVD, Blu-Ray, and streaming showed a steady progression of technology that all impacted on cinema-going audiences. As M. J. Simpson says, neither Stanley nor Rigby "appeared to be aware of *I, Zombie: The Chronicles of Pain*. Or *The Eliminator*. Or *Demagogue*. Or *Sacred Flesh*. Or *Blood*. Or *Project Assassin*. Because they weren't looking in the right place. Cinema didn't just happen at cinemas anymore. The genre's future was in the Virgin Megastore, not 'All this week at The Royal'" (13). This new wave of

British horror *did* look back to the past, but in many ways, it was to the more violent movies of Pete Walker and his "Terror Films," in which the mundanities of the real world revealed the true horror of British society, that this revitalized approach took. Films that were once seen as "Hammer Gothic" (with its trappings of the castle on the hill, familial madness, and the traditional monster prowling the forest), like Pete Walker's *House of Whipcord* (1974), proved that there was power in critiquing British culture in more forceful ways than Hammer dared attempt. By adapting some traditional tropes of the "traditional Gothic" (for example, the castle becomes a block of public housing, and vampires become corporate businessmen), modern British horror filmmakers ensured that their horrors morphed into areas now classified as "Urban Gothic," "Rural Gothic," "Hoodie Horror," "Suburban Gothic," and even "Corporate Gothic," all of which transplanted the horrors of yesteryear straight into the horrible world of postmillennial trauma.

It is this postmillennial Britain that forms much of the backdrop to the revival of the modern British horror film. As the new millennium approached, the influence of it became apparent. The end of the century and the end of days was reflected in the fin de siècle attitudes of the previous century. This mind-set created an apocalyptic outlook. Blockbusters like *Independence Day*

(Roland Emmerich, 1996), *Titanic* (James Cameron, 1997), and *Moulin Rouge!* (Baz Luhrmann, 2001) may seem poles apart, but their themes of excess, death, and destruction—all capped off with terrific visual style—form a sense that things are ending and that despite optimistic endings, the destruction of all things is only a whisker away. Horror filmmakers used this fin de siècle approach at the very heart of their films. The Japanese film *Ring* (Hideo Nakata, 1998) focused on the destruction of the individual within society. Hollywood's *End of Days* (Peter Hyams, 1999) took this idea further and to its logical conclusion, where the conflict between good and evil finding its ultimate battle between Arnold Schwarzenegger's suicidal cop Jericho and Satan himself (Gabriel Byrne) is suitably spectacular and satisfying.

For Britain, the influence of the new millennium could not be escaped. The end of the world created a mind-set that focused on both the apocalypse of everything and of the individual, as seen in such films as *28 Days Later* (Danny Boyle, 2002). As Forshaw argues, the rise in popularity of vampire movies such as the *Twilight* saga captivated a new and younger demographic (165). There was a *need* for horror films to reach out and explain to this audience that changes in both their physical and emotional desires could be explained through the fantastical narratives they watched. As such, horror films—which had been so reliant on the genre conventions of the past—now began to mutate into newer, more audience-relevant forms.

Forshaw argues that part of the pleasure for a Gothic horror audience was that the tropes of the genre remained both in situ and embroidered and expanded on in different ways (165–66). Hammer had stagnated, unable to adapt to the changes in society. Modern audiences wanted to see and experience *some* of the tropes they had been used to, but they likewise wanted to be presented with something new and *challenging*. By the millennium, the genre was ripe for reinvention. While such elements as victim, monster, and Grand Guignol approaches were usually in evidence, the reliance on these forms meant that horror films gradually and persuasively swept over a passive audience that was used to seeing (and accepting) the same narrative tropes repeated from film to film. However, the better British horror films made cogent and interesting points about Britain at the turn of the century. According to Forshaw, the modern British horror film is among the surest of winning genres (167). With the films beginning to move away from the "traditional" Gothic stories and incorporating such realistic elements as business ethics, recession, and the bleak future of the country's underclass into their narratives, the United Kingdom's horror-film output remains healthy. This approach of taking these ideas that affect every corner of the country proved an excellent method in deconstructing and critiquing the Britain of the new millennium. Such films as *Severance* (Christopher Smith, 2006), in which a business-training course led by an unethical American conglomerate ends in barbaric violence, and the public-housing-set *The Disappeared* (Johnny Kevorkian, 2008) are at polar ends of the British horror canon, but they (and many others discussed in this book) use contextual societal elements as backdrops against which their horrors play out. They *question* the moral and ethical climate of a Britain undergoing (violent) change.

This change has been manifest across all areas of the modern British horror film. Forshaw notices that there is a provocative mix of banal modern-day living and gruesome mayhem in the films (184–85). Whereas the savants of the past may have been Van Helsing dispatching Count Dracula, for the modern British horror film, they become people drawn from the target audience's demographic. These new heroes and villains may seem ordinary on the outside but are capable of the most violent acts on their victims. This means that violence is all pervasive and therefore *everywhere*. Films like *Salvage* (Lawrence Gough, 2009), *The Reeds* (Nick Cohen, 2010), *Sightseers* (Ben Wheatley, 2012), and *Tower Block* (James Nunn and Ronnie Thompson, 2012) may have been set in a middle-class cul-de-sac, seaside, countryside, or public housing block, respectively, but these locations clearly suggest that the Gothic horror locales of yesteryear have changed to become the norms for today's horror outings. Due to this new approach, in which Wales, Scotland, Northern Ireland, and England form the backdrops to the modern British horror film, the idea that Britain can only provide parochial films that are difficult to export to overseas markets is now redundant. Many of the new wave of films have become box-office successes elsewhere (for example, Neil Marshall's *The Descent* [2005] made $57.1 million on a budget of £3.5 million), which shows that, like Hammer had done years before, British horror films can compete on an international stage.

Hammer Films, resurrected in a blaze of publicity, tested this international platform in a fairly innovate way. Its online series *Beyond the Rave* (Matthias Hoene, 2008) and direct-to-DVD thrillers *Wake Wood* (David Keating, 2009; UK/Ireland) and *The Resident* (Antti Jokinen, 2010) dipped their toes into blood-drenched waters some years before it garnered huge box-office receipts with the Daniel Radcliffe star-vehicle ghost story *The Woman in Black* (James Watkins, 2012). These tentative steps forward may mean that Hammer Films is here to stay, but only time will tell. Indeed, it is really only the sobriquet of Hammer Films that remains resolutely "British," and the work of

Matt Hills shows that while the company has branched out into theater and literary areas, the actual "identity" of the company remains stuck between producing films that reflect the present and simultaneously wanting to be loyal to the company's past heritage. However, the fact that *the* name of British horror has been resurrected shows just how vibrant the marketplace is.

With filmmaking becoming relatively cheap through advances in digital technology, lightweight cameras, and off-the-shelf editing software, filmmakers of the post-millennium have been given greater freedom to both make and distribute their films than before. Filming on location is easier than in the past. Special effects and makeup effects are viewed on digital platforms immediately. Likewise, the numerous platforms that launch these new productions, including websites, horror film festivals, direct-to-DVD releases, pay-per-view streaming sites, crowd funding, local and regional initiatives, and social media, all help to push the latest films out to a wider audience.

That does not mean that all productions reach an audience. While a few individual titles such as *28 Days Later* and its superior sequel, *28 Weeks Later* (Juan Carlos Fresnadillo, 2007), *Dog Soldiers* (Neil Marshall, 2002), *The Descent*, and *The Woman in Black* found large audiences primarily due to their larger budgets, canny marketing strategies, and word of mouth, many films fell into relative obscurity. However, their importance to the canon of the modern British horror film cannot be sidelined. The vast array of movies under the catchall umbrella title of "British horror cinema" is mostly genre fare, but they all have something *British* about them. This might sound obvious, but the films discussed in this book reflect life and/or attitudes in Britain, and despite coproductions such as *Severance* being partly funded and filmed in Europe, there is an overriding "feeling" of Britishness about them.

The subjects of this new panoply of horror are diverse. There were traditional ghost stories like *The Dark* (John Fawcett, 2005), *The Awakening* (Nick Murphy, 2011), and *Soulmate* (Axelle Carolyn, 2013). Zombies lumbered around in *The Abandoned* (Nacho Cerda, 2006), while the £45-budget *Colin* (Marc Price, 2008) stood as a comparison to the $28 million *Pride, Prejudice and Zombies* (Burr Steers, 2016). Otherworldly horrors from beyond space tormented their victims in *Evil Aliens* (Jake West, 2005) and *Attack the Block* (Joe Cornish, 2011), while vampires, werewolves, and serial killers bit, ripped, and stalked their prey in *The Witches' Hammer* (James Eaves, 2006), *Howl* (Paul Hyett, 2015), and *Fox Trap* (Jamie Weston, 2016), respectively.

The most frightening monsters were undoubtedly human. The hoodies of *Eden Lake* (James Watkins,

2008), the killers of *Blooded* (James Walker, 2011), and the torture-porn lovers of *The Cutting Room* (Warren Dudley, 2015) reflected the most base of human depravations. On a lighter note, *Shaun of the Dead* (Edgar Wright, 2004), *Cockneys vs Zombies* (Matthias Hoene, 2012), *Grabbers* (Jon Wright, 2012), and *Nina Forever* (Ben Blaine and Chris Blaine, 2015) dealt with zombies, alien invasions, and vampiric immortality with a genuine sense of the joie de vivre about them. While many of these horrors were set in the "real" world and with "realist" approaches, there were also art sensibilities afforded to the horror film: *Berberian Sound Studio* (Peter Strickland, 2012) was an attempt at unraveling both the complexities of sound composition and the human mind through the making of an Italian *giallo* thriller, while *Byzantium* (Neil Jordan, 2012) was an ode to the Euro-vampire thrillers of the 1970s. Unfortunately, despite good reviews, neither film was particularly successful at the box office.

With the advent of cheaper and more readily available technology, modern British horror directors like Neil Marshall, Christopher Smith, Johannes Roberts, and Jakes West began to craft their films first at home and then through film schools. For filmmakers like Jason Impey, film festivals and exploitation-tilted production and distribution companies helped get their films exhibited. Companies such as Brain Damage Films, Pendulum

Pictures, and Chemical Burn Entertainment specialized in promoting zero-budget films as part of "collections" available at knockdown prices to a discerning clientele. Simpson singles out Jason Impey's work as an exemplar of this trend, with his films *Sick Bastard* (2007) and *Home Made* (2007) coming under some scrutiny (159). A quick glance at Impey's credits on the Internet Movie Database shows that his films total eighty-eight, an impressive achievement by anyone's standard. But with most of his films having titles like *Naked Nazi* (2008), *Necrophiliac: The Lustful Dead* (2015), and *The 12 Slays of Christmas* (2016), it is doubtful they will see the light of day in "respectable" cinemas. Their release at horror-film festivals, on DVD, and on streaming sites shows that there are individuals out there who love working in the medium knowing full well that there is an insatiable appetite for a particularly discerning horror audience that is fed up with seeing sanitized horrors from major studios.

It could be argued that that mainstream (horror) audiences and critics remain ignorant of the rebirth of horror postmillennium, much as they were when Hammer et al. were in the throes of their own financial successes. Despite the odd review of a bigger-budgeted (and therefore "important") horror film appearing in the columns of daily newspapers or film magazines like *Sight and Sound* and *Total Film*, the more dedicated horror aficionado is more than likely to look to publications such as *Fangoria*, *The Dark Side*, and *Rue Morgue* for information about the latest splatter gorefest. Likewise, flagship film programs hosted by "important" film critics would never discuss movies such as *Demons Never Die* (Arjun Rose, 2011) and *Strange Factories* (John Harrigan, 2013). This is because *true* British horror cinema, that which tugs at the very sensibilities of British cultural life, not only is arguably difficult to track down but more importantly questions the very fabric of Britain as a postmillennial country that is now on the verge of possible economic and social collapse in a post-Brexit world. It is *this* approach to the horror film that makes the modern British horror film both fascinating and "difficult" for many people to comprehend and appreciate.

Johnny Walker's excellent overview of contemporary British horror film focuses on how the genre has been revitalized through both changing audience tastes and distribution patterns. According to his figures, while there were relatively few horror films in the 1990s, in postmillennium Britain, there was an explosion of horror titles. Walker says that by the end of 2010, more than four hundred titles had been registered and released across a variety of media platforms. At the end of 2014, at least another one hundred had appeared. This incredible number of films, from a genre once clouded and dogged by controversy from the popular press and moral guiders of British society, clearly showed that there was—*is*—a genuine need and appetite for British horror films to reflect and comment on British society *of the moment*. Walker points to certain factors that helped this genre revival: changing domestic tastes and critical attitudes, cheaper platforms, easier production and distribution of micro-budgeted films, more funding opportunities through private investors, tax relief, and grants and other subsidies from the UK Film Council.

All of these are relevant. But what remains at the heart of the British horror film's tremendous revival—and one that should be both applauded and celebrated in equal measure—is simply this: although the films may not have the budgets, casts, crews, marketing, and distribution platforms of their American cousins or the critical appraisal afforded to Japanese horror, what they do have is the ability to engage and critique the society in which they so obviously belong. It is *this* that makes the modern British horror film so important in both reflecting the insularities of British cinema and offering a critique of the country that moves it away from a costumed period romp, a realist drama, or a middle-class comedy, which constitute much of mainstream British cinema. These horror films have an ability to engage with their audience while (un)subtly and (in)directly reflecting the undertones of a divided and fractured society. In a time of radical change, when pre-/postmillennium optimism has turned to the potential threats of economic collapse from a government focusing on divisive policies, including the frightening folly of Brexit, the British horror movie remains energetic, stimulating, and vibrant. *This* is why they should be studied, and this is the purpose of this book.

The book is divided into three separate areas. Chapter 1 investigates the rise of "Hoodie Horror" as seen through three frightening and thought-provoking movies. Chapter 2 discusses the idea that the great outdoors is anything *but* great. The chapter analyzes movies set in the forest, at sea, and in caves, and these three very distinct locations become psychogeographically linked to both their narratives and their characters. Chapter 3 reveals how the monster *out there* is really the monster *within* us all. Each chapter has a semiformal structure, purely for ease of use. All chapters provide a general overview of a particular subgenre, with each giving context as to how the films reflected their relative construction. With the overview forming the background to each chapter, space has been given to an in-depth analysis of three movies that the author thinks remain exemplars of the relevant area under study. A cast list is provided, and a variety of different reviews have been taken from "traditional" film critics, highbrow and populist newspapers, and fan sites. This has been done to show that, in the era of the Internet, fan forums remain an active part of celebrating the modern British horror film.

This book is not exhaustive. Not all British horror films are mentioned. The list of the films at the back of this book will, no doubt, have some that are missing. Likewise, the films chosen as exemplars are purely subjective.

When multiplexes show the latest Hollywood blockbuster across seven screens and hard-earned cash has been wasted on a film that panders to the most easily satisfied of film audiences, perhaps the main point of this book will then become apparent. It is written to get people interested and stimulated in seeking out these grim, grisly, and horrible movies. It is also to show the importance of the modern British horror film as a movement that reflects back to its audience the day-to-day horrors of today's Britain.

Above all else, this book was written for you to enjoy. I hope you do.

1

THE HOODED TERROR

In 2011, over a period of five hot and humid days in August, numerous cities in England underwent a period of genuine civil unrest. A supposed incident in the Tottenham suburb of London, in which police allegedly shot a suspected youth gang member, sparked a series of riots that soon spread from the capital to the Midlands and was widely reported in both UK and European news bulletins.

As Johnny Walker suggests, there were two key views as to why these riots became a symbol of a disenfranchised (primarily youth) "underclass" within Britain's social structure (85). As early as 1990, Charles Murray had written that there was a distinct separation of this "underclass" from the rest of the majority of the UK populace, which followed over ten years of divisive Thatcherite, Conservative right-wing rule. Imogen Tyler (2013) suggests that the rise in gang culture, knife crimes, and inner-city violence was the result of this burgeoning cultural group becoming synonymous with both an unwillingness to work *and* being prone to using violence. Mass-media reports clearly blamed young, working-class people for the riots.

However, the disenfranchisement of this supposed "underclass" came to symbolize a culturally fractured Britain, in which it was becoming more and more apparent that poverty-stricken areas, low employment, poor infrastructures, failing educational establishments, and a lack of genuine opportunities for people in need provided the backbone and impetus for demonstrating the cracks running throughout the country. While the demonstrations were, as Walker points out (85–86), originally peaceful, the intervention of gangs and opportunists spiraled into five days of chaos, anarchy, and tension, reminiscent of the riots in Birmingham, Brixton, Toxteth (1981), and Broadwater Farm (1985) almost thirty years before.

With the media in full-on aggrandizing mode, one group of individuals were singled out for attention. They wore tracksuits and T-shirts and face-hiding hooded sweatshirts. These "hoodies," as they became known, were apparently a cultural by-product of "broken Britain" but in reality came to symbolize the right-wing media's view of everything that was anti-Conservative. When the *Daily Mail* reported that "streets, town centres and shopping malls do not properly belong to us and the hoodie [is] symbolic of those we fear have taken over" ("Under

That Hoodie"), it was only a matter of time before savvy filmmakers would use this background of a splintered society to begin to question the moral fabric of a country fraught with tensions. And what better way to do it than through the horror genre?

As with any subgenre, it has to have a beginning. While earlier films such as *The Damned* (Joseph Losey, 1963) and *Quadrophenia* (Franc Roddam, 1979) offered depictions of a growing and dissatisfied youth culture in Britain in the postwar years and punk era, respectively, their modest links to the terrors of today's movies can be seen. When comparing the teddy boys, mods, and rockers of yesteryear to the hoodie, Jane Graham's article in the 5 November 2009 edition of the *Guardian* pointed out that hoodies

don't have the pop-cultural weight of the other subcultures, whose members bonded through music, art and customised fashion. Instead, they're defined by their class (perceived as being bottom of the heap) and their social standing (. . . as being oppositional). Hoodies aren't "kids" or "youngsters" or even "rebels"—in fact, recent research by Women in Journalism on regional and national newspaper reporting of hoodies shows that the word is most commonly interchanged with (in order of popularity) "yob," "thug," "lout" and "scum."

According to the media, Britain had become the target of feral gangs intent on destroying everything not like them. Walker suggests that the first "hoodie horror" has its origins in genre films like *Donkey Punch* (Oliver Blackburn, 2008), *Harry Brown* (Daniel Barber, 2009), and *The Reeds* and *Travellers* (Kris McManus, 2011), which do not have hoodies in them per se but rather have young protagonists that create/react to violence (89–90). However, the art-house film *The Great Ecstasy of Robert Carmichael* (Thomas Clay, 2005), with its controversial, static single-shot rape scene, and the football-hooligan movie *The Football Factory* (Nick Love, 2005) do have hoodies and began to show the symbiotic link between the character and violence, with the garment symbolic of them both.

Arguably the first film to have a *direct* impact on the "hoodie horror" subgenre is the claustrophobic Euro thriller *Ils* (David Moreau and Xavier Palud, 2006), with its story of a young teacher and her husband who are terrorized in their own house. This persuasive film never reveals the motivation for its horrors, and the perpetrators remain anonymous until the last few frames of the movie. It was this enigmatically frightening approach to the hoodie that separated the European from the British oeuvre. For example, the *Ils* poster's huge close-up of an eye remains ambiguous at best, whereas the poster for *Cherry Tree Lane* (Paul Andrew Williams, 2010) shows a black background, an open cottage doorway with flowers growing around it, a blood-stained set of handprints on the door, and a hooded figure with his back to the viewer, which immediately sets up both the atmosphere and the narrative of the film with some force. If one takes the poster of *Cherry Tree Lane* as an exemplar of the advertising of the cycle, it becomes apparent that with the stark warning of "No warning. No mercy. No escape" and media comments such as "the ultimate urban horror" and "visceral, brutal, terrifying" screaming out at the spectator, the "hoodie" became synonymous with terror and violence. When coupled with the popular press calling youths "feral," "louts," "chavs," "yobs," and "evil," the "hoodie" automatically became a stereotype linking the films to their contextual world, where hoodies were portrayed as hanging around street corners, drinking, threatening, and creating fear for "ordinary" law-abiding citizens, much in the same way that Marlon Brando's and James Dean's teenage rebels had done in the 1950s (Bawdon; qtd. in Walker 88). While Matthew Turner would see the hoodie (both garment and wearer) as "a signifier of moral decline, ASBO culture and a general social downward turn." James Murray, Dave Robbers, and Matt Drake's inflammatory right-wing article "Should Hooded Youths Be Banned from Our Streets and Shops?" portrayed hoodies as rampaging gangs that brought terror and menace to the streets of the country, putting at risk the moral majority who wanted to be left to their own peaceful lives.

Interestingly, these peaceful lives were placed into two distinct locales: the (inner/working-class) city and its (middle-class) suburbs, and the countryside. When Andrew Higson wrote of "That Long Shot of Our Town from That Hill" (153), he romanticized industrial landscapes, rows of factories, terraced houses, cobbled streets, washing lines, gunnels, and wash houses, helping to create a sense of contextual, nostalgic, and romantic "identity" within a film's themes. Movies such as *Heartless* (Philip Ridley, 2009), *F* (Johannes Roberts, 2010), *Cherry Tree Lane, Citadel* (Ciaran Foy, 2012), *Comedown* (Menhaj Huda, 2012), and *Community* (Jason Ford, 2012) used the town/cityscape as areas of urban decay. While these films may begin with a skyline shot of London (as an example) with its landmarks both cementing the film into its geographical position and orientating the audience, they then proceed *inward* to the *psychogeographical* aspect of the films. That is, *we* experience the city *through* the eyes of the character(s). By using stock locations of everyday life, such as the high-rise, the public housing project, the school, and the shopping center, the horrors on display in these movies offer a genuine sense of concrete credibility because they *look* authentic, while also accentuating the often-implausible narratives into a form of believability.

As an alternative to Higson's view, hoodie horror's infrequent trips to the countryside, or at least areas of nature and parkland, reveal the flipside to the view that Britain is a green and pleasant land. By setting the film in a rural context, these country hoodies carried on where films such as the American *Texas Chainsaw Massacre* (Tobe Hooper, 1974) and the British *Straw Dogs* (Sam Peckinpah, 1971) left off. The main characters usually leave the comparative safety of the city only to be confronted with the smell, look, and feel of an alien environment. In *Community*, the run-down rural housing project is the place of nightmares, where the clashing juxtaposition of cultures blossoms into unrelenting violence. In *Eden Lake*, which will be analyzed further in this chapter, the countryside transforms from a place of beauty to one of threats and violence. It is this conflict of philosophies, outlooks, and morals that brings the two geographical and psychogeographical elements into sharp collision.

Whichever way the "hoodie" was seen, whether the films were set in the city or the countryside or in the day, night, or twilight hours, shrewd filmmakers used hoodies as a driving force in their movies, reflecting and commenting on the Britain of the new millennium. In order to both contextualize and critique hoodie horror as a genuine component of the modern British horror film, I now briefly analyze three movies.

Heartless was director Philip Ridley's first film since *The Passion of Darkly Moon* (1995). The film made its debut at Film Four's FrightFest (2009) and got a cinematic release on 21 May 2010. The main cast comprised Jim Sturgess (Jamie), Joseph Mawle (Papa B), former *Doctor Who* companion Noel Clarke (A.J.)—himself an exponent of inner-city living with *Kidulthood* (Menhaj Huda, 2006), *Adulthood* (Noel Clarke, 2008), and *Brotherhood* (Noel Clarke, 2016)—Clémence Poésy (Tia), Nikita Mistry (Belle), Luke Treadway (Lee), and guests Timothy Spall (George Morgan) and Eddie Marsan (Weapons Man).

The film uses the story of *Faust* as its base. Jamie is a lonely and troubled but likable photographer. At twenty-five, he is still a virgin, blaming a heart-shaped birthmark that covers half his face for his failure to get a girlfriend. At his studio, he meets an aspiring model, Tia, who is shocked by his facial disfigurement. As Jamie develops a set of photographs of buildings, he notices a lizard-like face peering out from one of the windows. Walking home, he sees a group of these lizard creatures standing around a fire. They turn and walk toward him, revealing huge, razor-sharp teeth. Over the course of a few days, more and more reports about Molotov-cocktail murders are reported in the neighborhood. The demonic gang attacks Jamie and his mother, setting her on fire. As Jamie recovers in hospital, he receives a phone call from Papa B, a man he has dreamt about. Papa B offers him a lifeline of Faustian proportions. Papa B tells Jamie that he will remove the birthmark from his face *if* Jamie carries out one act of violence for him.

The film garnered a mixture of both positive and negative reviews. Gary Goldstein enjoyed the film, calling it "a compelling psychological horror-thriller [that] contains a tremendous amount of heart." He praised Jim Sturgess, calling him "a terrifically watchable presence": his performance was both "moving and deeply sensitive." Goldstein also found the overall atmosphere, plot, and direction compelling, "even at its most seemingly outlandish." Kyle Smith gave a backhanded compliment to the movie. He felt that it was "an uneasy mix of B-movie shocks, social commentary and sentimentality" that contained "several delicious examples of Ridley's macabre wit." However, perhaps the review from Ben Rawson-Jones for *Digital Spy* is the most waspish: "*Heartless*? Gormless is a more apt description . . . thoroughly dull protagonist . . . more pathos for meat in a butcher's shop window . . . form and content are desperately terrible."

Despite this bashing, the film went on to be nominated for Best Film at the Sitges Film Festival (2009) and the Melies Award at European Fantastic Films Festivals

Federation (2010). It won the Silver Melies Award at the Leeds International Film Festival (2009) and the Vision Award for Best Independent Feature Film at the Toronto After Dark Festival (2010), while Fantasporto awarded the film its Grand Prix, Best Director, and Best Actor accolades (2010).

The performance of Jim Sturgess is strong, and Jamie has been written and performed in such a way as to elicit sympathy from the audience. The director has assembled a good and believable cast. Timothy Spall plays Jamie's father in his usual gentle, melancholic style, while Eddie Marsen's all-too brief appearance as Papa B's henchman remains a highlight of the film.

Ridley used his own compositions on the soundtrack (with his collaborative partner, Nick Bicât), which acts like a Greek chorus that both comments on the action and draws in aural links among the film, its characters, and the audience. Sturgess sang two of the film's songs, with both him and Ridley seeing them as reflecting Jamie's state of mind at various points of the film's narrative.

While gore is minimized, two standout scenes remain genuinely disturbing. The first sees Jamie meeting Papa B in a run-down block of flats. The neon-lit walls are covered in dregs, and the floor is filthy. Papa B gives Jamie his ultimatum: do one work of chaos, and the birthmarks will disappear. Jamie succumbs to this temptation. Papa

B gives him a Molotov cocktail; Jamie lights it, drops it to the floor, and is engulfed in flames. When the flames subside, Jamie slowly peels off his charred skin to reveal his new identity. As he unpeels his old self from his new, the skin both bubbles and cracks. The second, more aggressive sequence sees the return of Papa B, as Jamie cowers from him on a rooftop. Papa B calls to one of his reptile minions, who hands him A.J.'s head. A.J.'s eyes flicker open, and he screams in terror. Papa B lifts the head to his mouth and bites two huge, bloody chunk of flesh from A.J.'s cheek. Whereas Jamie's killing of a male prostitute is blackly comedic, these two scenes remain horrific because not only are they treated with seriousness, but through the terrific combination of overbearing sound, lighting, and editing, the horrors for Jamie (and us) become all too apparent.

There are two very distinct ideas behind *Heartless*. The first is that the film offers a point of view that then–prime minister David Cameron's "broken Britain" was not just the result of societal breakdown but arguably stemmed from the individual within that society. The film positions the hoodie as both *Other* and *Us* in distinct ways. Jamie wears a hoodie, and as his face is covered, he is technically a terror to society: he is *Other*. However, he also has a respectable, entrepreneurial job, lives with his mother, pays rent, is polite, seeks love, and strives for friendship:

James is therefore *Us*. This duality remains at the core of the movie, in which Jamie crosses these borders with a mix of both pain and ease.

Like the monstrous, crawling, albino subhumans of *The Descent*, *Heartless*'s monster-hoodies are feral, violent, lizard-like creatures that use their hoodies to mask their reptilian features. They roam in packs, make shrill shrieking noises, and have sharp teeth, thus becoming the *Other* that terrorizes *Us*. *But* the normal-hoodies are also shown to be the kids of millennial normality: they play loud music, get shouted at by older members of society (who probably listened to music just as loudly), use the language of their generation, and remain part of a culturally familiar component of contextual Britain. When the mass media's view of hoodies portrayed them as "wild packs of yobs" (Collins), whose "frightening, surreal and carnivalesque" (Tyler) nature caused them to be catalogued between the divide of "normality" and "otherness," it becomes obvious that the hoodies not only symbolize the idea of a "broken Britain" but are also emblematic of it. It is these two viewpoints that lie at the heart of *Heartless*.

The second idea is that Ridley made the cityscape an integral part of the film's overall meaning. There are establishing shots of London, including the City, the River Thames, and other ubiquitous heritage icons such as red double-decker buses and black taxis. However, when Ridley backs away from these tourist trappings, the London of heritage becomes what Peter Hutchings calls "London Horror," which had been seen before in such movies as Michael Reeves's *The Sorcerers* (1967), Pete Walker's *Cool It, Carol!* (1970), and Alfred Hitchcock's *Frenzy* (1972).

The film's opening scene is of nighttime London, where the bright lights of the city pierce the darkness. As the camera pans down to focus on a housing project, the sounds of cars, police sirens, and a voice shouting "You're gonna fucking die!" bring the viewer sharply *into* the film. The lingering shots of lights flickering on and off in row upon row of apartment buildings, mixed with shots of the city, offer life and hope. But these are pushed away, changing to empty side streets, where rubbish is piled high up against graffiti-strewn walls. This is the London that tourists *don't* see, and by focusing on these side streets (themselves becoming an allegory for horror films as being on the periphery of "acceptable" genre), the narrative removes the tourist trappings, replacing them with a locale that remains both ordinary and normal, while simultaneously corrupting and frightening.

While Jamie's experiences appear to be hallucinatory and brought on by the constant bombardment of anti-hoodie news reports, the *psychogeographical* aspects of the city directly affect him and therefore *us*. The audience views the city through Jamie's experiences. The suburbs are clearly frightening, badly lit, crumbling, inhospitable spaces through which the residents and the hooded terrors roam. Jamie photographs the derelict, empty, crumbling buildings as part of a hidden London, but in reality, they resemble numerous urban landscapes up and down the country. These inhospitable places become a representation not just of Britain but of Jamie himself. Like the crumbling edifices surrounding him, Jamie remains both empty and broken. He has become marginalized. The connotation is that society has failed the working classes of the past and, by doing so, has created those of the present. This viewpoint is compounded further when the hooded demons of this fictional narrative become (and reflect) the stereotypes perpetuated through the eyes of the media in the *real* world. The chavs, youths, louts, yobs, scum, and hoodies created by the media in *Heartless* are lizard monsters, themselves forming an allegory for both Jamie's state of mind and the underclass of millennium Britain. It would appear that *Heartless*, with all the connotations that this title brings to its audience and its subject matter, is a critique not only of certain aspects of modern Britain but also of the media, through which these hallucinations have become manifest.

The film *F* received its world premiere on 27 August 2010 at Film Four's London FrightFest. With a low budget of £150,000, this lean, seventy-nine-minute shocker remains a stunning critique both of Britain's school system and of the fractures of familial and married life. The director, Johannes Roberts, assembled a renowned cast, including David Schofield as the English teacher, Robert Anderson; Eliza Bennett as his daughter, Kate; Juliet Aubrey as Helen, his estranged wife; Ruth Gemmell as the head teacher, Sarah Balham; and Emma Cleasby as Lucy, the school's librarian.

Robert Anderson, an English teacher at Wittering College, North London, gives a pupil an "F" grade for his essay. The school's politically correct policy is that students should never be given this grade but rather an alternative "RS" (resubmission) mark to avoid confrontation among the school, the education authority, the student, and the student's parent. When the student sees his grade, he head-butts Anderson in the face, and the school governors force the teacher to take three months leave so as to calm down the situation, for the pupil to leave, and for Robert to reassess his life and his teaching. Robert remains deeply affected by this incident and is concerned about the lack of solidarity shown to him by his peers. His marriage is in tatters (his estranged wife, Helen, has taken their daughter, Kate, to live with her), and he has no respect from either of them. His colleagues dislike him, and his pupils do not want to be taught by him.

Robert's return to work remains fraught with tension. His headmistress hates him, and when he sends a memo to all of the employees of the school that highlights the rise in bullying and violence against teachers, he is called delusional and paranoid. As Robert oversees his daughter's detention, he argues with her over the use of her mobile phone. He slaps her and immediately regrets it. Over the course of the next hour, he sees hoodies outside the school. Finding that the school telephone lines have been cut, and after he has a near miss when a bottle containing the message "U R Dead" is hurled through a window at him, Robert realizes that he and the school are under attack.

As with the majority of these hoodie horrors, there was a mix of both positive and negative reviews of the film. Anton Bitel's musings for *Little White Lies* thought that it "effortlessly converts Noughties anxieties about the generation gap into genre thrills, while bringing an unusual psychological resonance to all the breathless cat-and-mouse" tropes of the genre ("*F*"). Peter Bradshaw of the *Guardian* felt that is was an interesting thriller that had a "shrewdly chosen, contemporary theme." He felt that it may have been better served to flip the scenario so that "those faceless demon-hoodies [who] seem to belong to a more supernatural kind of thriller" would themselves be subjected by "the teacher . . . to a siege ordeal," which would more than amply demonstrate the power of the themes being explored ("*F*").

Lizzie Duncan's review for HorrorNews.net was decidedly against the movie. While she saw that the film addressed some of the very contemporary issues facing UK teachers, she felt that the idea of the middle class's fear of youth culture was dealt with in a "superficial nature." Any attempt at realism (seen through handheld camera movements and the employment of numerous close-ups) was dissipated with the "supernatural and otherworldly" treatment of the hoodies. Her main argument was that Robert's character remained unlikable, and because of the distancing of him from the audience through his alcoholism and violent behavior toward his daughter, there was little opportunity to actually sympathize with him. Charles Gant's *Variety* review summed up this critique, by arguing that the "film's focus on the grizzled lead protag, rather than the agile adversaries closer to its target aud's age, may prove a commercial misstep," even though "green-tinged lensing provides a unifying, if oppressive, aesthetic, while the sparse, haunting score, incorporating sinister choral elements, make the grade."

When the B-movie "base under siege" flick *Assault on Precinct 13* (John Carpenter, 1976) used a police station (in itself a container and begetter of violence) as its main locale, the inability of the forces of good and order and the unending attacks by unknown assailants struck a chord with Americans' desire to break free from the stigma of both the Watergate scandal and the Vietnam War. Fast-forward over thirty years later, and Johann Roberts's excellent *F* has taken Carpenter's basic premise and given it a distinctly postmillennial British twist. In this instance, the symbolic use (and eventual devastation) of the police station as a sturdy and protective representation of law and order has been replaced by a symbol of future hope (and similar destruction) in the form of the school. The jaded American police officer becomes the jaded, alcoholic teacher. The vicious hoodlums of South Central Los Angeles become the faceless, hidden hoodies of North London.

David Cameron's inflammatory article for the *Telegraph* on 2 September 2007 categorically stated, "To fix broken Britain we shall start at school." The opportunistic Conservative MP (and future British prime minister) argued that "four in every five youngsters receiving custodial sentences have no qualifications. More than two-thirds of prisoners are illiterate. And nearly one third of those excluded from school have been involved with substance abuse" (qtd. in Walker 105). This scaremongering tactic, typical among politicians trading on hot-off-the-press topics, was designed to pinpoint schools as failing in their remits under the then-Labour government.

Johannes Roberts, already a tried and tested horror-film director with *Sanitarium* (2001), *Hellbreeder* (2004), *Forest of the Damned* (2005), and *When Evil Calls* (2006), used Cameron's polemic as a springboard to present a film in which the school becomes a site for violence rather than education, and one that clearly demonstrates the fractured division between the people *in* authority (the teacher) and those wanting to *take* authority (the hoodie). Even within those areas of power, there are divisions. The majority of staff members dislike Robert, the police are easily divided and killed, and the film's climax sees Anderson sacrificing the love of his daughter to save her, while his wife enters the school, in which the hoodies are hunting.

Anderson is first seen with his back to a class of disinterested pupils. As he reads extracts from *King Lear* to them, they shuffle in their chairs, look at each other, and ignore him. His monotone voice bores his pupils, and in a foreshadowing of future events, he tells them that Lear "loses his kingdom, . . . his daughter, . . . all through his own folly." As he turns to the class, the words "The Fool" are on the blackboard immediately behind him. In that instant, he has become both Lear and Fool and, like Lear, is sent on a downward spiral before any possible redemption. When Robert says, "Unfair is when something happens for no reason," he prefigures his own fate at the hands of his student protagonists, much in the same was as Lear's own kin betrayed him.

Walker argues that Anderson is not a wholly sympathetic character (105–7). His behavior toward his pupils, both through belittling them and then especially after hitting his daughter, clearly demonstrates that he is justifiably *blamed* for his actions but unjustifiably faulted for not following the school's PC procedures of awarding the appropriate essay grade. The audience is pushed into a position of identification with Robert, despite his hitting his daughter. He becomes a victim of the very society that he is helping to maintain. This society has seen him ridiculed by his colleagues and goaded into slapping his daughter (for which there is no defense); the head teacher, Sarah, says "Goodbye Anderson" to herself when phoning one of the governors about his behavior, the security guards dislike him, his marriage has collapsed, and Kate ignores him. As he wanders aimlessly through the corridors, which in turn become a labyrinth through which there is seemingly no escape, where teaching staff look at him with disdain and his pupils constantly mock him, the walls of Robert's mental state begin to collapse around him.

But through all this, Robert's moral compass does not waiver. He tries to save everyone trapped in the school. When Robert begins to take Kate to the hospital, fully knowing that Helen has entered the building on the way to her grisly doom, the film's positioning of Robert becomes clear. With a choice to face, Robert decides his, Helen's, and Kate's destinies with little hesitation. The wife remains sealed to her fate. Kate *may* redeem her father through time and forgiveness. For Robert, who has become both awkward hero *and* villain, despite his break-down, alcoholism, and inner violence, there is the hope of a possible future redemption, which will only transpire when the brutal attacks on the staff and the two police officers become apparent. The fact that he will (presumably) be questioned over leaving Helen to her grisly fate remains tantalizingly unanswered. For the audience, the fact that they have been party to Robert's horrific experiences, in which sides have been taken, remains a satisfying coda to this terrific shocker.

To follow on from Carol Clover's arguments that much of horror is set within a "Terrible Place," it becomes obvious that the school, which should be a bastion of moral and educational enlightenment, becomes—at least for Robert—a place of genuine horror and tension. This horror manifests itself in numerous ways. There are long shots of empty, dark corridors, with broken lockers, cracked tiles, and shadows encroaching on all the characters. The school transforms into the modern-day equivalent of the Gothic castle on the hill or the haunted house at the end of the street. A young, attractive PE teacher is stalked through the gym and beaten to a pulp in the locker room, her jaw ripped open and her skin flayed; the librarian, who earlier states, "Some kids don't deserve to be in school," is killed among her own bookshelves; the caretaker has his throat slit while cleaning a classroom; the headmistress is butchered and her lifeless body propped up on her office's leather chair, which in itself becomes symbolic of her loss of authority over the pupils; and a security guard is set on fire after being locked in a large refuse bin. The fact that these locations have been used in such violent ways not only emphasizes the idea that *nowhere* is safe but becomes bleakly and blackly comedic by having their traditional uses radically overturned to become horrible places of death and destruction.

While there have always been divisions between the people who are in authority and those who are not, the schoolroom has usually been depicted as a place of enlightenment. In the case of *F*, this idea is totally reversed. Kate smiles when given an A grade for her assignment. However, this enlightenment stops abruptly when Robert berates a pupil for a poor piece of homework. When the pupil hits him, the division between teacher (authority) and pupil (not authority) begins, in which the horror of not just working but *being* in the school affects Robert's confidence. This division becomes more apparent when staff members also rebuke him: the security guard ignores him; a caretaker says, "You look like shit"; teaching staff regard him with nothing but suspicion; the school governors agree with the parents' view of his belittling their child; and the headmistress finds fault in his teaching methods at every given opportunity.

This division is taken further when Robert returns to work. The school's labyrinthine structure, coupled with his fragile mental state, forms an obstacle for his mental and physical well-being. It manifests itself as a site of inner turmoil and outward struggle, where both physical and metaphorical menace lurks around every corner. Returning to Clover's view that the school becomes a "Terrible Place," it is, as Walker states, bound to the "(unhealthy) preservation of a family unit" (106). This unhealthy symbiotic linkage, in which the family unit is constricted and constrained by the oppressive walls of the school, here manifests itself in purely *negative* ways. The school and its inhabitants dismantle Robert both as an individual and through the collapsing ethos of education.

Kate's transition from angelic daughter to the disrespectful, badly behaved, promiscuous teenager that David Cameron would have removed from the streets of broken Britain is indicated through both her physical and emotional transformation. With her ponytail swapped for unruly hair, knee-length school skirt replaced by a miniskirt, makeup covering her fresh-faced innocence, and both kissing her boyfriend and smoking in front of her father, Kate becomes a skewed form of allegorical metaphor for the perceived downward spiral of "agreeable" moral behavior and general moral decline that Cameron insisted was in evidence in postmillennial Britain. Even at the end of the film, when Kate lies dying in Robert's arms, she says that she will never forgive him for abandoning her mother. The message is clear: the younger generation *still* berates members of the older one for their own failings, the failings of their parents, and the failings of an educational system that cannot steer them toward a life away from depravation and lost hope.

The hoodies are presented in much the same way as in *Heartless*. They are seen as primal, animalistic, violent, and pack-driven creatures. They climb bookcases, shelves, and walls with apparent ease, swiftly and almost silently creeping up on their victims. The framing of the hoodies continually emphasizes their distinct "Otherness." While there are shots of them as individuals and within groups, their features are *never* revealed, even when in a close-up in which two hoodies stand over a dying police officer, with the camera tilted up at them. Likewise, they are never *quite* shown in focus and often stand on the very edge of the frame, teasing both the characters and the audience with their threat of violence. This not only

gives them a genuine sense of the supernatural, the macabre, and the uncanny but also renders them *not*-human,
with a complete lack of morals and lack of "identity, as
their hoods obscure both their sex and their nationality"
(Walker 106).

This is an interesting point on which to conclude this
analysis of this superior shocker. Richard Garner suggests
that the nonspecificness of both gender and nationality
in these "monsters" lends a genuine sense of strength to
the idea that the hoodies here are just that: *monsters*. But
these are not the traditional monsters of the Gothic but
rather monsters perpetuated by the media in the Britain
of the postmillennium. This is what makes the hoodie,
and *F* in particular, all the more frightening. The fact that
the hoodies remain completely *unknown, hidden, non-
gendered*, and *nonnationalized* makes them arguably *the*
terror of the modern British horror film.

James Watkins's terrifying *Eden Lake* was shot over a
period of six weeks in the summer of 2007 in and around
Black Park and Frensham Ponds, the former stomp-
ing ground of Hammer Films. It was first shown at the
Cannes Film Festival on 15 May 2008 before getting its
UK release on 12 September 2008. It earned $3,983,997 at
the US box office. The cast was strong. Kelly Reilly and
Michael Fassbender play a likable middle-class couple,
Jenny and Steve; Jack O'Connell is the feral Brett; Thomas

Turgoose is the frightened Cooper; Jumayn Hunter plays the vicious Mark; and the ever-reliable Shaun Dooley plays Brett's father, Jon.

Jenny and Steve take a weekend drive into the countryside and head toward the town of Redcott and the nearby Eden Lake. Steve says that he had visited the place during his youth. While the two settle down at the lakeside, a group of teenagers arrive and play their music loudly. Steve asks them to turn it down, but they refuse. Following an argument, he accidentally kills the gang's dog. The kids puncture the tires on Steve's car and then turn their violence toward him and Jenny.

The film has often been seen as the tent pole of the hoodie horror genre. On release, it garnered mostly positive reviews. Denis Harvey's column in *Variety* drew some comparisons between *Eden Lake* and the American *Saw* (James Wan, 2004). Harvey wrote that Watkins's first feature has "duly grisly content but is (mostly) credible enough to avoid a rote exploitation feel." He went on to say that the film "doesn't feel like torture porn so much as a rural-jeopardy thriller *in extremis*" and complimented both the acting of the film's leads and its excellent production values. Alex Hess, in his review for the *Guardian*, recognized that the hoodie horror genre was a genuine British phenomenon and said that the film was "one of the most brutally terrifying experiences in [his] film-watching life." He also pointed out that the "best horror is borne of real-life societal fears" and that *Eden Lake*'s "hard-edged realism" of broken Britain showed how the sort of "reactionary conservatism that you define yourself against is actually within us all."

Hess's fellow critic Peter Bradshaw exclaimed that *Eden Lake* was "the best British horror film in years: nasty, scary and tight as a drum." He also felt that the film was a "violent ordeal nightmare that brutally withholds the longed-for redemptions and third-act revenges." For Bradshaw, it remained "a nihilist scream and a vicious satirical twist in our perceived social wounds: knife-crime, gangs and the fear of a broken society" (*"Eden Lake"*). The right-wing *Daily Mail* columnist Christopher Tookey took this idea even further. He called it "a first-rate British horror film that taps into our deepest fears and offers a thought-provoking insight into such topical subjects as knife crime and gang culture," feeling that it was an intelligent film, which "fulfilled two purposes of horror: it involves you emotionally and it's frightening."

Without a doubt, *Eden Lake* is an intelligent, frightening, and genuinely disturbing entry in the hoodie horror cycle. Watkins had cut his teeth as a screenwriter on the thriller *My Little Eye* (Marc Evans, 2002), and Working Title, which had released the earlier film, saw that he had talent and asked him to develop a number of his own screenplays, including *Gentleman Thief* and *Lonely Planet* for the company. The latter eventually ended up as an Australian Outback road movie called *Gone* (Ringan Ledwidge, 2007), but Watkins was unhappy with the ultimate changes to his script and, when he renegotiated his contract with Working Title, insisted on an opt-out clause that his screenplay called "Little Terrors" would come under his direction if optioned. Watkins took the script to *The Descent*'s producer, Christian Colson, who commissioned it, provided that Watkins could show his directorial skills by lensing a ten-minute Cornwall-based version of it.

When Colson stepped away from producing *Eden Lake*, Richard Holmes, best known for producing the comedy *Waking Ned* (Kirk Jones, 2007), told that he thought the premise was strong, had resonance in Britain's contextual climate, and was engagingly structured (Simpson 266). Having Michael Fassbender and Kelly Reilly attached to the project certainly helped convince Holmes to greenlight the movie. Watkins insisted, "I'm not making a social realist drama. It's an all-out genre piece. But I want *Eden Lake* to contain a modern resonance and intelligence above the thriller norm" (Simpson 266). This "modern resonance" took shape in two ways: first, though the idea of the countryside becoming a genuine place of horror and terror, and second, by demonstrating the growing social divide between the two thirty-something middle-class professionals and their housing-project opposites.

There have been numerous rural horror films, in which the forest has become a site of torment. This remains a staple trope of many American productions: *Deliverance* (John Boorman, 1972), *The Texas Chainsaw Massacre* (Tobe Hooper, 1974), *Evil Dead* (Sam Raimi, 1981), the *Friday the 13th* series, and especially the horrors set in and around the Black Hills of Maryland in *The Blair Witch Project* (Daniel Myrick and Eduardo Sanchez, 1999) and its sequels. All rely on the "outsider" (in these instances, city folk) trespassing into areas in which they are simply not welcomed by the "insider" community.

For the United Kingdom, with its much-smaller geographical area, the importance of setting horror in the wild woods remains just as potent and important for the genre. Horror films like *The Wicker Man* (Robin Hardy, 1973) and *Wilderness* (Michael J. Bassett, 2006) certainly rely on the landscape as a place in which their horrors can unfold. As Carol Clover suggested, the narrative trajectory of the city (and, therefore, civilized) folk entering into the countryside, in itself a completely alien environment to them, means that they are *not like* those in Britain's green and pleasant land. Rather, the city and city folk are *we* and the countryside and country folk *not we*: a rural *Other*.

What makes *Eden Lake* so fascinating is the way that the countryside has been filmed. The film's superb photography shows the rural beauty of the woods both as welcoming and as a signifier of encroaching danger and menace. When Jenny and Steve arrive at the lake, all is calm and serene: the sun shines; there are light, fluffy clouds up above; and the water is warm and inviting. However, once the teenagers arrive, storm clouds appear on the horizon, the air gets chilly, and the lake water becomes uninviting. For Jenny and Steve, the lake turns from a veritable Eden into Hell. It becomes the place of nightmares (after all, city folk are really only used to living in the concrete jungle), while for the hoodies, it remains a playground through which they can torture the unlucky yuppie Adam and Eve.

This dynamic is most telling in the scene in which Steve is tied up with barbed wire to a fallen tree trunk. The hoodies stand around him, punching and kicking him until his face and body are a bloodied mess. The group takes it in turns to torment him, each one taking a knife and plunging it into his torso. One of the gang runs the blade lovingly across Steve's face before stabbing him twice. Brett forces the youngest member of the coven, Cooper, to stab Steve in his tongue. As the young boy walks away, Brett takes some of Steve's blood and smears it on Cooper's face, echoing the traditions of the country hunts of the upper classes. Jenny looks on helplessly through the undergrowth. The scene is uncompromisingly brutal. The hoodies whoop, cheer, laugh, cajole, and celebrate Steve's destruction. As Jenny tries to phone the police, the gang locate her through her mobile's Bluetooth signal. As she turns and runs, with the gang in pursuit through the ferns, the quick edits, terrifically thunderous music score, and framing of both Jenny running through the maze of paths, trees, and bushes and the hoodies riding their bikes to catch up with her are breathtakingly exciting.

Therefore, it becomes obvious that the countryside of *Eden Lake* and the housing development seen at the beginning of the movie—which promises "Executive Homes, . . . a secure gated community of fifty superior new England homes . . . with 300 acres of woodland"— will eventually succumb to the terrifyingly real threat of both the woods and the inhabitants of Redcott. The wild things that the housing company wishes to tame will eventually eat the staid and suburban middle classes who have bought its properties.

From a social standpoint, it must be remembered that the BMX-riding children of Redcott cannot vote and that their only moral guidance has been from the fractured families of Tony Blair's time as prime minister. M. J. Simpson calls them "a generation raised from infancy with constant messages about rights and no mention of responsibilities" (267). In conjunction with this interesting point, Walker argues that the very name of the town, Redcott, suggests birth, blood, and horror linked to the infant's bed (100–102). Therefore, the kids of *Eden Lake* cannot escape their "blood lust" through either any (lack of) moral guidance *or* the fact that they are "surrounded" by its subliminal connotations. While these subconscious messages are the result of the children's physical surroundings, their vicious attitudes toward outsiders stem directly from their families. The working-class families of Redcott are shown as threatening to anyone outside their community and as not accepting their children being blamed for anything. They form part of an almost inbred community that does have a warped sense of communal togetherness, in which people look after one another and help one another. However, they also have no genuine sense of moral right and wrong. For the families of *Eden Lake*, ground down first by over ten years of social disintegration through the Thatcher years and then by the "blame culture" of the Blair years, fracturing their moral sense of right and wrong, there is no genuine socialistic-utopian collective community. Rather, the Redcott inhabitants have become insular and self-gratifying, while only really wanting to protect themselves from the outside world.

This mind-set comes to a head in the final sequence when Jon drags Jenny into the public-housing bathroom, and he peer pressures his family into both hiding their secret and getting other fathers to help him kill her. He slaps his son, Brett, who looks on blankly, which echoes his own treatment of Cooper when he coerces him into stabbing Steve earlier in the film. As the bathroom door shuts quietly, Jenny's screams fade into the distance. The last shots of Brett deleting the videos of the kids torturing the couple, which are then followed by him putting on and removing Steve's Ray-Ban sunglasses while looking at his reflection, clearly show the filmmakers' intentions. The horrific violence against Steve and Jenny becomes a by-product of broken Britain's domestic spheres up and down the country. While it is justifiable to argue that the teenagers of *Eden Lake* (and, therefore, everywhere else in the United Kingdom) have been demonized, the older generation reveal themselves to be just as vicious as the offspring they have created. After all, as kids, the older generation would have behaved badly, too. But in *Eden Lake*, both working-/under-class generations openly seek to destroy those who are not like them, while the middle classes cannot, despite their attempts at "understanding" them, do anything to "keep a handle on them in spite of supposedly 'knowing better'" (Walker 106). It is this that makes the film so impressive an achievement.

Without a doubt, the hooded terror remains an extraordinary aspect of modern British horror cinema.

By taking the Gothic *Other* of yesteryear and planting it directly into present-day Britain, films such as *The Children* (Tom Shankland, 2008) and *Citadel* begin to critique British society in a way not seen since the "troubled teenager" movies of the 1950s and '60s. The hoodies of the first decade of the twenty-first century were extensions of the white-T-shirt-wearing, rebellious youths of the documentary *We Are the Lambeth Boys* (Karel Reisz, 1959), the bikers in *The Leather Boys* (Sidney J. Furie, 1964), and even the Hells Angels of *Psychomania* (Don Sharp, 1972). Many of these "teenage rebellion" movies have a fractured family at the heart of the narratives. The hoodie horror is no exception. Entries like *The Children* and *Community* have no "family" in the traditional sense of love, warmth, and kindness but rather push the idea of "family" into areas of violence or bloodshed.

This lack of the conventional human element was extended further into the locales of these hoodie horrors. The streets of the city were never paved with gold but were horrid, filthy, and squalid places, where anonymity among the masses was guaranteed. James Leggott's work on horror suggests that a recurring characteristic of the British horror film is when the stranger moves from a place he or she knows to a hostile and unfamiliar landscape. Peter Hutchings calls this unfamiliarity "uncanny landscapes." He argues that they have become a part of the lexicon of the horror film (and, really, the Gothic novels of the past), that they become almost de rigueur through their overuse. Both Leggott and Hutchings seem to suggest that the landscapes of the "traditional" horror film (usually a *mittel*-Europe of pure fantasy) will always remain hostile and places of *Otherness*. For the hooded terror films, this can idea be taken further. The woods that once surrounded Dracula's castle have become the encroaching signifiers of doom around the backstreets of London, the inbred community of Redcott, and the suburban Wittering College, and the Dracula, Frankenstein, and Wolf Man of the European-set horrors of the past have mutated into becoming the hooded terrors within today's British society.

By placing these hoodie horrors into a contextualized broken Britain, we can see that the locations of these horrors and the individuals or groups within them remain inextricably interlinked. The streets of inner-city London are shown as all encroaching, and the feral gangs that roam the streets are by-products of their lack of community and traditional family units, where the only "family" they know is of the violent gangs to which they belong. The college of *F* becomes a site of destruction rather than education, where the only lessons learned are by the adults who are tortured and killed. The community of Redcott remains a very broken one and one that cannot—and will not—see its fractured, inbred society be destroyed.

These hoodie horrors may be glamorizing and demonizing the faceless youths of Redcott et al., so that they become commentaries on how the media portray the "yobs," "youths," and "louts" on every street corner, from which no middle-class person is safe. But it could also be argued that they are simply making a statement about the "broken Britain" of today, much in the same way as the "teenage problem picture" had done some fifty or sixty years before in America. However, what they all do is posit the idea that unconstrained violence toward those who are "not like" by those who "are like" is part and parcel of living in a country that has gone through turbulent years of social upheaval and media manipulation. It becomes readily apparent that in the case of the hooded terror film, *nowhere* is safe in postmillennial Britain.

2

THE GREAT OUTDOORS

As discussed in chapter 1, the geographical and the psychogeographical aspects of both the location and the individual remain an important component of the modern British horror film. For the hoodies, the city was their breeding ground for violence. The high-rise buildings, public housing, run-down estates, rubbish-strewn streets, dimly lit alleyways, and locked-away secrets meant that the everyday became a frightening commentary on British life in the twenty-first century. Even the countryside of *Eden Lake*, with all its connotations of fresh, pleasant living, was just as corrupt, with rural folk seeing the city ones as easy prey.

It was obvious that the great outdoors of Britain's once green and pleasant land remained a threat to everyone who thought it could be tamed. The traditional Gothic novel used the landscape as an important structure within its narrative. In the early works of Horace Walpole and Ann Radcliffe, the main protagonists often took journeys into the exotic, wild, and vivid landscapes of a nonexistent *mittel*-Europe. These landscapes were bleak, harsh, and desolate. They were sexually enticing, violent places where the Englishman (or woman) abroad was very much the alien in the European midst. Ann Radcliffe's proto-Gothic novel *The Mysteries of Udolpho* (1794) transported her heroine to the hot, eroticized, marginalized regions of southern Europe. In Bram Stoker's *Dracula* (1897), the lawyer Jonathan Harker travels to central Europe and the Carpathian Mountains and, once there, finds himself trapped within the labyrinths of the ancient ruins of Castle Dracula.

These far-off lands and their craggy landscapes were far removed from the "safety" of a civilized England. While the landscape of Emily Brontë's *Wuthering Heights*, with its vast heathlands and ferocious storms, may have been romanticized, Dickensian London, with its billowing chimneys, vast factories, workhouses, cobbled streets, slums, and tenements all within throwing distance of one another, provided an insight into the developed landscape of a post–Industrial Revolution Britain. But the landscapes of both West Yorkshire and London were *British*. Therefore, they were *safe*.

In relation to the psychological or psychogeographical processes involved in the Gothic (and therefore film) genre, the journey into these landscapes came to represent such things as life cycles, desire, sexuality, fragility, and death. Settings such as the sea, the sublime mountains, ruined castles, haunted woods, wastelands, cliff tops, and blasted heaths assumed heavily symbolized and determined meanings directly linked to complex psychological readings of both the character and the narrative.

Mary Shelley's Gothic classic *Frankenstein*, in which she describes the landscape of Orkney as "desolate and appalling," was one of the first of its type to accentuate both the dangers and the horrors found lurking among the forests, ferns, and heathers of a wild and windy countryside. For the Gothic writer and the later filmmaker, the landscape became an uncanny site of anxiety and alienation. The desolate countryside of the horror film transformed a sustainable link between *us* and *it* (where the countryside provided both home and food) into a place that haunted, undermined, threatened, and transformed *us* into the wild animals *it* also supported.

British filmic horror always used the landscape as a form of metaphor and allegory. Films like Hammer's *The Mummy* (Terence Fisher, 1959), *The Reptile* (John Gilling, 1966), *Plague of the Zombies* (John Gilling, 1966), and *The Witches* (Cyril Frankel, 1966) employed the colonial cultural sphere of influence to transform the English countryside into a place of brooding sepulchral atmosphere. The exoticism of the "foreign" that invaded these locations may have embodied the social and political anxieties between England and its colonial dominions during the eras in which they were set, but they also reflected the collapse and disintegration of the British Empire and its resultant transformation into the Commonwealth in postwar Britain.

Those British horror movies that used locations that did not employ "foreignness" but instead used "Britishness" directly found their home in two distinct locales: the town and the countryside. The city, especially London during the Swinging Sixties and Dour Seventies, provided the backdrop to such "modern-day" horror settings as *Twisted Nerve* (Roy Boulting, 1968), *Virgin Witch* (Ray Austin, 1971), *Death Line* (Gary Sherman, 1972), and *Straight on Till Morning* (Peter Collinson, 1972). The journey from the dangers of the city to the supposedly bucolic countryside was no barrel of laughs for the protagonists of *Mumsy, Nanny* (Freddie Francis, 1970) and Pete Walker's *Frightmare* (1974) and *House of Whipcord* (1974).

The modern British horror film used the cityscape well: those movies discussed in chapter 1 clearly used the city as a constricting, deadening place of violence. While the zombie *28 Days/Weeks Later* movies treated the landscapes as spectacular places of alienation and the hoodie horrors focused on the collapse of the working classes, an oddity such as *London Voodoo* (Robert Pratten, 2004) used an interesting premise (a wealthy and ambitious analyst relocates his family from New York to London, where his wife becomes possessed by an ancient voodoo spirit) as a critique of the wealthier members of London's upper classes. In other words, no one was safe. The city was not, therefore, the romanticized view of "That Long Shot of Our Town from That Hill" (Higson 2), where someone would turn and look back toward a city that is both wonderful and romanticized. Rather, it was a place that offered the surface glint of success while dragging its inhabitants down into its sewers.

Those British horror movies that used the countryside to contain their horrors found a home in such "folk horror" as *Witchfinder General* (Michael Reeves, 1968), *Blood on Satan's Claw* (Piers Haggard, 1971), and *The Wicker Man* (Robin Hardy, 1973). All of these offered contemporary spins on New Age religion and the youth culture of their time within a countryside landscape removed either to the past or to the outer islands of a remote Scottish community. Even the "foreign" invasion of two American tourists in *An American Werewolf in London* used the English rhubarbing villagers of Yorkshire both to emphasize the tourists' American-*Other* and to hide the villagers' inbred-*Us* shame. The irradiated landscapes of British science-fiction/horror hybrids such as *Quatermass II* (Val Guest, 1957), *Village of the Damned* (Wolf

Rilla, 1960), *Island of Terror* (Terence Fisher, 1967), and *Doomwatch* (Peter Sasdy, 1972) also showed how the once-peaceful country village had become a place where the death and destruction of the individual, the community, and the wider populace remained a constant threat. This idea found its way into children's educational films, too. The public information film highlighted the horrors of living and working in the countryside: the apocalyptic *The Finishing Line* (John Krish, 1977) had children playing "chicken" on a busy railway line; and the remarkable *Apaches* (John Mackenzie, 1977) clearly demonstrated that farm and rural life was both a dangerous and a foreboding place (Shail). Nowhere was safe in rural Britain.

However, this threat didn't just apply to the land. The sea, with its undulating, pulsating, and unstoppable tides and currents not only enticed sailors to their watery graves but also brought up creatures from the depths in such films as *Gorgo* (Eugene Lourie, 1960) and *The Lost Continent* (Michael Carreras, 1968). A film like the oil-rig set *Parasite* (Andrew Prendergast, 2004) may have seen its crew fending off an alien, a dreadful script, awful CGI, and poor acting, but it made other oil-rig movies like *Proteus* (Bob Keen, 1995) and *The Devil's Tattoo* (Julian Kean, 2001) seem like high art in comparison.

However, two seascape horrors stand out. With a premise based on the exploitation flick *Tower of Evil*

(Jim O'Connolly, 1972) and using the iconography of the superior ghost story *The Fog* (John Carpenter, 1979), *Lighthouse* (Simon Hunter, 2000) was a gripping, creepy, and stylish killer-on-the-loose movie. Starring James Purefoy, Rachel Shelley, Chris Adamson, and Don Warrington, the film was promoted as a thriller along the lines of the Antipodean movie *Dead Calm* (Philip Noyce, 1987). Reviews were mixed. Kim Newman called it "a conventional slasher movie" that "fails to live up to its own hype"; Stephen Holden's *New York Times* review called it a "grade-C British horror thriller [with] crude pretensions, . . . extremely gory, with severed heads flying in all directions," while Scott Grantham of *Video Watchdog* felt it was "one of the scarier and more suspenseful slasher flicks to emerge from the flotsam of direct-to-horror-video." What made the film rise above others of its type is simple: the narrative was compelling, the acting strong, and the suspense palpable.

While the second seascape horror, *For Those in Peril* (Paul Wright, 2013), may have been a box-office dud due to its limited release, the story of Aaron, a young misfit who survives a strange boating accident, remained an intriguing, chilling, and genuinely striking calling card for its writer/director, Paul Wright. Filmed in and around Gordon, Aberdeenshire, the film boasted an extraordinary performance by George MacKay, utilized velvety cinematography, and provided a sensory experience in which the audio and visuals combined to provide something often disjointed and contradictory but simultaneously thought provoking for the viewer.

Back on dry land, *The Hole* (Nick Hamm, 2001) saw four private-school friends finding an abandoned World War II bunker ripe for exploration. The film had an excellent production design, claustrophobic atmosphere, and a young Keira Knightley to unsettle the viewers. Neil Marshall's lycanthrope reinvention *Dog Soldiers* had it all: good action sequences, *proper* werewolves that stood on their back legs to chase and attack their prey while their long claws shredded the flesh of their victims, a terrific cast (including Sean Pertwee and Liam Cunningham), a jolt of black humor (a soldier uses a staple gun and sticky tape to stop his guts from spilling out), a thunderous music score, and excellent cinematography to hammer home its genuine shocks. With the soldier and base-under-siege themes intact, *The Bunker* (Rob Green, 2002) and *Deathwatch* (Michael J. Bassett, 2002) were both interesting, though flawed, attempts at providing a crossover between the psychological horror of Val Lewton's 1940s chillers and soldiers-under-pressure war movies. Likewise, the grim *The Seasoning House* (Paul Hyett, 2012) catalogued the depths to which human depravity would sink, presenting a genuinely unrelenting view of horror that was all far too real to be considered escapist entertainment.

The Scottish Tourist Board's promotion of tartan, kilts, bagpipes, Edinburgh, and a beautifully wild and rugged landscape may have been helped by the inexplicably lauded *Trainspotting* (Danny Boyle, 1996), but the following films were certainly *not* on its advertising websites: *The Last Great Wilderness* (David Mackenzie, 2003), *Wild Country* (Craig Strachan, 2005), *Wilderness* (Michael J. Bassett, 2006), *Sawney: Flesh of Man* (Ricky Wood, 2013), and *White Settlers* (Simeon Halligan, 2014). Each showed the highlands as a home for werewolves and cannibals who roamed with abandon. Other regions of this sceptre'd isle fared no better. Wales was the setting for the spiritual and supernatural horror of *The Dark* (and Jake West's daft *Evil Aliens*). Two other notable regional horror films included the outrageous black comedy *Sightseers*, which showcased the horrors of cannibalistic caravaners, and *The Borderlands* (Elliot Goldner, 2013), which provided frissons of ghostly delight with its "found footage" scenario of church diabolism and something lurking in the crypt.

As with *Eden Lake*, the vast expanses of woodland found around Britain's national parks became sites of horror in the strong *Forest of the Damned*, while Hammer Films' low-budget *Wake Wood* was a fair financial and critical success, despite its being on the shelf since 2008. As a strange, not entirely successful follow-up to the director's own *The Wicker Man*, Robin Hardy's confused and lackluster *The Wicker Tree* (2011) showed that lightning could only strike once in particular areas. Arguably the most successful of these forest horrors was the fast-paced thriller *A Lonely Place to Die* (Julian Gilbey, 2011), in which a woman is pursued through the landscape of the Scottish islands by a group of Serbian killers.

When the city folk moved into the countryside, all hell broke loose. One such oddity included *Dust* (Adam Mason, 2004), which was summed up by its director as a chronicle of what happens when wayward London twenty-somethings culturally collide with a family of insane pig breeders. *The League of Gentlemen's Apocalypse* (Steve Bendelack, 2005) was a thoroughly self-indulgent, blackly humorous follow-on from the surreal TV series, which commented on the in-bred problems of small-town living in Royston Vasey. The clash of city and country folk formed the cornerstone of the bleak comedy *The Cottage* (Paul Andrew Williams, 2008). *Small Town Folk* (Peter Stanley-Ward, 2008) may have captured the in-bred shenanigans of people living in the town of Grockleton, but the film remained far too limited in scope, budget, and ideas to make any sort of statement other than that this outing contained nothing but clichéd stereotypes and narratives.

It would appear that the use of specific locations will always remain a vital part of the horror film. Britain has not been alone in this, though. American exploitation films of the 1970s used the dusty backwaters and byways to house their own types of horrors. Films like *The Last House on the Left* (Sean S. Cunningham, 1972), *The Texas Chainsaw Massacre* (Tobe Hooper, 1974), *Race with the Devil* (Jack Starrett, 1975), and *The Hills Have Eyes* (Wes Craven, 1977) used their locations as a dismal backdrop to their subjects. This influence of the American backwoods was well in evidence when Sam Raimi's *Evil Dead* and its first sequel used the forest as a force of evil in its own right. When a slew of both new horror outings and remakes in the 1990s and postmillennium used these outdoor backdrops, it became obvious that the American backwaters were not the place to be. Movies such as *Jeepers Creepers* (Victor Salva, 2001), *Joy Ride* (John Dahl, 2001), *Cabin Fever* (Eli Roth, 2002), and *Wrong Turn* (Rob Schmidt, 2003) and remakes like *Friday 13th* (Marcus Nispel, 2009) ventured into these dangerous territories but mostly as backdrops to the narrative—unlike the terrific *My Bloody Valentine 3D* (Patrick Lussier, 2009), in which the setting of an abandoned mine was crucial to the plot.

In Europe, the great outdoors was also used as a backdrop to horror. In France, Jean Rollin's lyrical use of the beach and castle in *La vampire nue* (1970) and *Les frisson des vampires* (1971) certainly paved the way for transplanting the horrors from the surreal to the real in *Haute tension* (Alexandre Aja, 2003), *Ils* (David Moreau and Xavier Palud, 2006), and *Livide* (Alexandre Bustillo and Julien Maury, 2011). Denmark's Lars von Trier's provocative *Antichrist* (2009) was played out against the mist-shrouded backdrop of a moodily lit forest. The icy and barren regions of Norway saw the narrative of *Troll Hunter* (André Øvredal, 2010) play out in blackly comedic tones, while Germany's *Du hast es versprochen / Forgotten* (Alex Schmidt, 2012) used the beautiful countryside of Thuringia and Saxony-Anhalt as its milieu.

What all these movies do is use these locations and plant their horrors directly into them. Through the use of the wilderness, the bleak and barren landscapes, parched deserts, scrublands, and forests, the all-too-real locales become an extra character within the narrative. The dry, desert highways of America may seem far removed from the lush forests of Germany, but they remain as important in creating atmosphere as the haunted house did.

The forests of *Severance*, the cave system of *The Descent*, and the high seas of *Triangle* become the physical backdrops to their own narratives, while simultaneously becoming characters within their own right. In the case of the two latter movies, these locations directly reflect the main character's emotional turmoil. While the human monsters of these films appear to be the enemy, where humans' inhumanity toward one another spurs on the violence, degradation, collapse, and disintegration of the individual and the group, the great outdoors is anything but great, and it serves as both a framework and a catalyst to the horrors played out within it.

Christopher Smith, as a follow-up to his monster-in-the-underground *Creep* (2004), swapped the cramped interiors of the London underground for the foreboding forests of eastern Europe to produce *Severance*, an engaging, gory, well-cast horror / black comedy. His cast was interesting and uniformly strong. Most known for a Cockney wide-boy persona, Danny Dyer played the magic-mushroom-eating, pot-smoking Steve; TV's 24 actress Laura Harris was the film's hero, Maggie; Bond villain Toby Stephens played the obnoxious salesman Harris; Andy Nyman's Gordon was a sycophantic groveler; Babou Ceesay's Billy was the epitome of calmness; David Gilliam played the firm's boss, George; Claudie Blakeley's Jill was a goody-two-shoes; and Tim McInnerny was the smarmy head of department, Richard.

The film's scriptwriter, James Moran, had been writing for years but with little noted success, until his script for

Cheap Rate Gravity won the Sci-Fi (now SyFy) Channel's shorts competition. The resultant short film was shown as a support feature to *Final Destination 2* (David R. Ellis, 2003) two years after Moran's proto-*Severance* script *P45*, about yuppies on a team-bonding exercise, was green-lit. As Moran recalled, he had been caught on a commuter train where "loads of pinstriped yuppie swine" had pushed past him and the others, used their mobile phones annoyingly loudly, and generally made a nuisance of themselves. Moran "realised that there was some interesting ground to cover by putting a bunch of ordinary office types into a slasher movie and seeing how they would react" (Simpson 201). The small, independent production house Qwerty Films optioned the film and approached Smith to direct. At first reticent and with no intention of working on another horror film after *Creep*, Smith found that he liked Moran's original idea and added his own notes to it. These notes included adding the war on terror and the idea that the arms industry had power without any form of culpable responsibility.

Funding was granted from the UK Film Council, N1 European Film Produktions, Isle of Man Film, Dan Films, and HanWay Films. The film was retitled *Severance* and shot over a six-week period from July to August 2005. Location shooting took place in both Hungary and the tax-friendly Isle of Man.

The plot is straightforward. Seven British employees of Palisades, a global arms manufacturer, are working in Hungary to sell their latest "tank-busting" landmines. As part of their duties, they are to take part in a team-bonding exercise at Palisades' brand-new forest lodge. When their bus stops on a small mountain road and their driver abandons them following an argument with Richard, the group walks through the forest and eventually comes upon a dilapidated and ramshackle building. Thinking this is part of the team-bonding exercise, they decide to stay the night. Jill spots someone spying on her and screams. When the team ventures outside, they find that high up in the surrounding canopy of trees are wire walkways that encircle the building. The following morning, Harris and Jill walk to find a phone signal but only find the bus driver lying face down in a small river. The others are paintballing, and as they take a break, Gordon gets his leg caught in a mantrap. As Steve and Billy struggle to get him free, Gordon's leg snaps off. At that moment, Harris and Jill bring the bus into view. They all get on board, but as they begin their escape, the tires are deliberately burst, the bus crashes and overturns, and a group of men begin to move out of the forest toward them.

Following press and sales screenings at Cannes, Munich, and London's FrightFest, the film went on UK general release on 25 August 2006. It was a solid financial success, making over $5 million at the box office. It was shown in New Zealand as part of a double bill with the horror comedy *Black Sheep* (Jonathan King, 2006). Reviews were mostly positive. Peter Travers felt that the film's "jolts are juicy" and that Smith was a dab hand at "mischievously blending *The Office* with *Friday the 13th*, keep[ing] things fierce and funny enough to give Steve Carell ideas." Both "Sean" and "Monkeyface" liked the film when reviewing it for *Internal Bleeding* (Aug. 2008). They singled out for merit its cast, the gross-out humor, and the fact that it wasn't a self-aware movie that winked at its audience in the knowing way so prevalent in other horror comedies. What they really loved was the fact that the film took its time in setting up its horrors, fleshing out the characters, and then delivering excitement with skill. Monkeyface gave the film a "solid 3.5 bloody machetes out of 5," while Sean awarded the film "4 bloody stumps out of 5," which was praise indeed.

Derek Elley felt that the film fully delivered its horrors in the second half and that the film's comic shock values were derived from the fact that no cast member was spared seeing the horrors unfolding on screen (*"Severance"*). Sam Toy's *Empire* review noted that horror and comedy were difficult to combine and that *Severance* was only partially successful, as "all too often the swing from humour deadpan derails it." As an antidote to this, the

Hollywood Reporter thought Smith had hit on a winning combination of horror and humor and predicted strong box-office figures (Bennett).

Tim Evans, in his review for Sky Movies, thought that the characters were sympathetic and the deaths ingenious and that the film had "three irresistible ingredients— 'sales team,' 'arms industry' and 'team-building' "—which were "concepts any right-thinking adults should despise." Philip French liked the film, telling his *Guardian* readership that "the comedy and horror are nicely balanced, and the cast is unusually strong" (*"Severance"*). Perhaps, as M. J. Simpson points out, it was Debi Moore who got to the heart of the film: she saw it as more creepy than comic, touching as it did on contemporary social and political issues and bringing the slasher and torture-porn fans something that was up-to-date and topical (204).

The blend of horror and comedy is a difficult juggling act. Get the horror too grisly or the comedy mistimed, and both fail. Get them right, and you have a winning combination. In the main, *Severance* falls into the latter category. Unlike *Shaun of the Dead*, the comedy here relies much more on the horrific situations that the team finds itself in rather than there being jokes (and *knowing* jokes at that) in themselves. For example, when Gordon's leg is snapped off in a metal trap, Steve runs to put the bloody stump in the bus's fridge. The leg is too big, and so Steve removes the boot and then the sock, all the while complaining not so much about the blood but about the foot odor. When this scenes follows the horrific snapping of the leg, with Gordon screaming in agony and the others looking on helplessly, the juxtaposition generates the laughter.

However, the comedy is then overturned when, five minutes later, as the bus lies wrecked on the mountain road, an unknown assailant decapitates Harris. As his head bounces down the road and stops, Harris looks back at his own bloody corpse and smiles. Following his earlier statement that Marie Antoinette saw her own lifeless body as her guillotined head looked up from the basket at it, Harris's own smugness shows that *he* was right, and so the last laugh is his. It is *this* that makes the humor so black. Arguably, the most outrageous jokes occur late in the film. When George uses a rocket launcher to destroy his assailants, he inadvertently blows up a passing passenger plane instead. During an assault, Steve rams a hunting knife up an assailant's rear end. As the man sinks to his knees screaming, Steve walks over to him and says, "Sorry mate, but this is gonna hurt." He kicks him, the man falls over, and the knife goes further up. There are no easy laughs in *Severance*, only black ones.

Though the basic story line suggests that the film is an isolationist horror movie, much in the style of *Deliverance*, the film makes its real impact in the subtexts and backgrounds to both the characters and the situation they find themselves in. The film begins with a jolting precredit sequence of George abandoning two young women to their fate as men chase them through the woods. George gets caught in a trap and is spun upside down. As the camera moves to a close-up of George and then spirals so that *we* can see what *he* sees, a soldier moves toward him/us. Taking out a huge hunting knife, the soldier stabs George, and thick blood oozes down his chest. The credits then roll, and the viewer is introduced to the team driving through the Hungarian countryside.

As with Smith's previous *Creep*, the backstory is only alluded to. The staff are employed by Palisades, a multinational arms conglomerate that sold weapons to the country during the Cold War. This is an interesting backdrop to use. Following the end of the Cold War, eastern Europe's borders were opening up to film crews looking for cheaper locations and studios to film in. The allure of filming in these "alien" environments meant that both the history of the location and the setting itself became an inspiration for films such as *Hostel* (Eli Roth, 2005), in which political and social instability created a resonance that remained authentic, emotional, and frightening for its audience. Therefore, *Severance*'s Hungarian, Slovakian, or Romanian backdrop (Richard can't tell where the lodge actually is), with its traditional tales of vampires, werewolves, and demons shunted aside to be replaced by Cold War horror stories, explores the idea that the real-life horror atrocities of the recent past become the cornerstone to the team's current problems.

This idea is reinforced when the team sits around the lodge's kitchen. Harris talks about the building being a pre–World War I insane asylum, a place where the inmates overtook the staff and killed them. Palisades' men arrived to gas the inmates, because "there's no reasoning with the mentally insane." One inmate survived and swore revenge on all of the company's workers. Jill says that there is some truth in this story but that it occurred during the 1990s at the tail end of the Cold War. She says that the lodge was a detention center for "soldiers who liked the killing a bit too much. They were lunatics. Wiped out whole villages. Burnt people alive. Put heads on spikes. They were savages. Well-trained savages." She tells the group that the soldiers' government locked these soldiers away and tried to recondition them, but nothing worked: "Some escaped, hid in some empty buildings but not for long. Obviously it wasn't Palisades that killed them. It was their government. But it was us who supplied the weapons." Steve tries to convince the group that the building is "a sex lodge" where sexually frustrated nurses looked after old, dying men. When a younger man "with a bit of bollocks about him" turns up in a white safari suit and looking just like Steve, the nurses turn their sexual attentions to him.

This whole sequence is fascinatingly constructed and is the best scene in the film. By breaking it down into three parts, Smith implies that each of the stories *does* have an element of truth to it. Harris pays homage to the old German expressionist horrors of both Caligari and Nosferatu, where the inspector looks like the vampire and the asylum belongs to the mad doctor. A piano score accompanies the sequence, in scratchy, silent black and white. The soldiers hiding in the woods could be the inmate's descendants. Steve's sex-fantasy version of events is shot like a 1970s British soft-core feature, with saucy, sexy nurses acting out his fantasies, almost as an antidote or light relief to the others' horror stories. However, Jill's narrative remains the most frightening and accurate. As she talks, the camera cuts to handheld, found-footage-style sequences of soldiers shooting at innocent people. One soldier shoots two corpses in the head. Another mocks an old man by blowing smoke over his face, tapping his head with his fingers, and then turning to smile at the camera, which freeze-frames on his sardonic smile. Images of dead bodies, the soldiers tormenting old men and women, and the detention center looming over them create a genuinely disturbing and haunting sequence that far surpasses the copious amounts of gore and suspense found later in the film.

This haunting aspect returns in the film's climax. When Maggie runs from the forest pursued by a soldier wielding a flamethrower, she discovers the real detention center. As she sneaks around the buildings, she passes a stockpile of boxes, each one carrying weapons and marked with Palisades' distinctive logo. The genuine horror isn't the soldiers and their insane bloodlust or the location that acts as a catalyst for the team's destruction. Rather, it is the idea that these horrors stemmed from the lack of accountability of arms manufacturers to sell their weapons to the highest bidder, where the rampant forces of capitalism have helped to create the very monsters in the forest that then turn back on their creators. This subtext cements *Severance*'s success as a genuinely engaging, blackly comic horror film.

For the majority of people, the daily commute to work, with its same scenery, unchanging songs on the radio, and similar cars passing by along the same monotonous route, remains a way of life. The only way to escape this déjà vu is to retire, move, or die. Christopher Smith's remarkable *Triangle* (2009) reminds the viewer of just that scenario. After a hiatus of three years, Smith's follow-up to *Severance* proved to be an intelligent, intriguing psychological horror thriller. The film was a coproduction between the

United Kingdom and Australia, received funding from the UK Film Council, National Lottery, Framestore, and the Pacific Film and Television Commission, and was made through Dan Films and Pictures in Paradise. Even though the budget was a strong but modest $12 million, which was mostly spent in designing and building the two-thirds-size replica of the film's ocean liner, it demonstrated the difficulty for independent filmmakers to get homegrown funding for their movies. However, Smith has delivered a strong entry into the canon, and the film certainly belies its low(ish) budget.

The film's premiere was at London's FrightFest on 27 August 2009. It was distributed by Icon Productions and released in the United Kingdom on 16 October 2009. The film had later releases in Belgium (30 December 2009) and Holland (21 January 2010) but did not get a release in America. The film made little impact at the box office, taking only approximately $3 million worldwide. This is a shame, as the film deserved a much-bigger audience than it received.

The title reminds the viewer of the mysteries of the Bermuda Triangle, a loosely defined area of ocean marking points between the coasts and islands of Florida, Puerto Rico, and Bermuda. Tales of ships and airplanes mysteriously lost—the most famous being the five TBM Avenger torpedo bombers that vanished on 5 December

1945—or vessels found abandoned and floating on the high seas have certainly created a genuine aura of mystery for the location. The cause for these disappearances has been attributed to many things, ranging from paranormal explanations to more-earthly ones such as compass variations, violent weather, methane hydrates, or simple human error. Smith taps directly into the paranormal interpretation of the area to produce a film that is genuinely beguiling.

The film's lead character, Jess, is played by the Australian actress Melissa George, who became a horror-genre stalwart through such movies as *The Amityville Horror* (Andrew Douglas, 2005), *30 Days of Night* (David Slade, 2007), and *A Lonely Place to Die*. Other cast members included the New Zealand actor Michael Dorman (Greg), Rachael Carpani (Sally), Henry Nixon (Downey), and a pre–*Hunger Games* (Gary Ross, 2012) Liam Hemsworth.

Jess is a single mother struggling to cope with her six-year-old autistic son, Tommy. She prepares to take him on a boat trip with her friend Greg, but when she gets to the harbor, she is on her own. Greg and his friends are already on board his yacht, *Triangle*. He asks where Tommy is, and she vaguely replies that he is in school, even though it is Saturday. As the yacht sets sail, Jess experiences a nightmare and wakes to find that the boat is heading into a storm. Overwhelmed by the violent storm, the craft overturns. One woman is drowned, and the others sit on the upturned hull waiting to be rescued. Out of the mist appears the vast 1930s ocean liner *Aeolus*. Jess sees one person on the ship looking down at them. They board the liner but find it deserted. Wandering around the ship's labyrinth of darkly lit corridors, they quickly get split up. Jess and Greg find a message carved in blood on a mirror telling them to go back to the ship's theater. When they get there, they and the others are shot at. Jess escapes and runs onto the deck. She looks over the side, only to see herself and the others on *Triangle*'s hull waving up at her, and she watches incredulously as another version of herself and her friends climb up onto the liner.

The film received mixed reviews. Derek Elley felt that George was "a *tour de force*," while the "rest of the cast is largely shot gun fodder, with only Carpani etching something of a character." He found that the "early reels are genuinely intriguing" but that the finished film "only makes some kind of sense on its own fantastic level" ("*Triangle*"). Nigel Floyd's review for *Time Out* singled out George's performance, calling it "fearless" and "credible"; she "grounds the madness in a moving emotional reality, even as her sanity is lost at sea." Lucius Gore's *ESplatter* review called the film "one of the most intelligent, thought provoking genre films in recent memory."

William Thomas's review for *Empire* felt that the movie was "a satisfying mind-twister, with an unexpectedly poignant pay-off." Philip French seemed enamored of the movie, writing, "It's creepy, atmospheric stuff and at every twist of this Mobius strip we wonder how Smith will keep things going. But he manages it with considerable skill and we leave his picture suitably shaken" (*"Triangle"*).

What sets this film apart from many others is its visual style. The film looks remarkable. The opening sequences are filmed in a realistic way, with normal and everyday colors used for Jess's house, the harbor, and inside *Triangle*. However, when the yacht leaves the harbor, the film becomes saturated in vivid color. The blues of the sea and the sky are incredibly vibrant, and the use of sunlight becomes a mix of blinding yellows and white. As *Aeolus* sails out of the blindingly white fog bank, its blood-red funneling belching out gray smoke into the overwhelmingly bright sky, the effect is both ghostly and dazzling. In contrast to this image and reflecting Jess's crumbling state of mind, the ship's corridors remain darkly lit. The constantly prowling camerawork suggests hidden dangers lurking around ever corner, reflecting Jess's increasing mental instability.

This fragility is emphasized by the way Jess is constantly framed. She is placed on her own in both confined and open spaces. This framing is then accentuated and imposed on the other characters, who rush out from the dark into the open spaces of the blindingly white deck. The effect becomes as disorienting for the audience as it does for the characters, which makes the film's style feel all the more confusing for the viewer.

The plot may seem straightforward, but the repeated-event story line makes compelling viewing. The narrative is an old chestnut: events recurring with little change, much like in the film *Groundhog Day* (USA; Harold Ramis, 1993). However, whereas that movie played on concepts of time travel in comedic ways, Smith's focus on the elemental and violent forces of the sea and individual makes for deeper readings. By grounding the film in the ancient Greek tale of Aeolus and his son, Sisyphus, the film plays out like Greek tragedy. Aeolus was Mount Olympus's Ruler of the Winds. His son, Sisyphus, offended the Olympians and was punished by having to roll a huge boulder up a hill for all eternity. Once the boulder reached the top, it rolled back down, leaving Sisyphus condemned to a life of purgatory and torment for his crimes against the Greek gods. This mythical story forms *Triangle*'s backbone. As with Sisyphus, Jess is forced to pay for her crimes—in this case, her mental breakdown and treatment of her son—and is forced to endure a life of replaying the same events over and over, with no respite, until the end of time.

The narrative ends on a genuinely chilling note. Jess finds herself washed up on a beach near her house. She returns home, discovering that a doppelganger is already there. However, Jess is not the heroine of the film at all. She slaps and shouts at her son for his behavior. The "original" Jess kills her *Other*-self and drives Tommy toward the harbor. The car hits a truck and rolls down the highway. Jess wakes up to find herself looking at both her own and Tommy's corpses. A black-clad cab driver asks her, "Can I give you a ride?" This man says he is "just a driver," but when the skies darken as he approaches, it becomes obvious that he is the Angel of Death. He tells Jess that no one can save Tommy. Jess replies, "Take me to the harbor," and so her nightmare begins again. This superb ending to the circular narrative may seem a cop-out resolution, but it is much more meaningful than that. It reveals either that Jess's emotional and physical breakdown is in her own head (at the moment of her death, she finally comes to realize the horror of what *she* is and so forces herself to go through the events as a self-inflicted punishment) or that she is being forced into a state of limbo by some paranormal (or even Olympian) interference, and her perpetual torment is her just reward.

When Louisa May Alcott, author of *Little Women*, said, "I am not afraid of the storm for I am learning to sail my ship," little did she know that these words would form the psychological backbone to Jess and her metaphorical link to both the *Aeolus* and Sisyphus. During childhood, children set out a basic set of precious and emotionally important ideas, which when linked to social upbringing makes them unique as individuals. If the metaphor of the *Aeolus* sailing calmly through the ocean becomes a metaphor for Jess's character development, it establishes Jess's transformation through the narrative. Her mental state is reflected in the ship: its sturdy keel keeps her mental alertness intact; the ship's ballast becomes Jess's goal of escaping back to Tommy; her moral (ship's) compass steers her mental and physical directions; the ship's rudder becomes Jess's steering toward her goal; and her final destination, a "place to steer toward," reminds her that her ultimate objective is to return to Tommy. It is with this goal in mind, that she can be reunited with her son, that makes her link to the *Aeolus* all the more important. The ship reveals it to never be *just* a ship. It never was a physical place, either. It becomes the inner workings of Jess's subconscious, which has now cracked and broken through her own inability to cope with the pressures of modern family life.

It is quite obvious that Smith's film is not just a simple ghost story, time-traveling narrative, or thriller. The mind-bending mystery of *Triangle* puts the viewer directly into that dreadful feeling of déjà vu that everyone experiences. This allusive terrain, a never-ending feeling of being trapped within a dream, has meant that the audience actually *becomes* a part of Jess's unending nightmare. The film remains an astonishing achievement and one that both bewilders and reveals more with each viewing through its own ambiguity. It is this logic-defying approach that makes *Triangle* such a persuasive horror film. When Jess takes her taxi ride back to the harbor, the driver asks if she will come back. She replies, "I promise." She has sealed her own fate. She has become Sisyphus, anchored to eternity through torment, suffering, and pain. It is this incredibly bleak ending, in which the twisted and fractured geometry of both time and space *within her own mind* spills out of the screen to envelope the audience that makes *Triangle* such a compelling triumph.

Neil Marshall's remarkable *The Descent* takes the viewer on a journey into the mind of a woman who has lost not only her family but also her own fragile grip on sanity. One year into developing his women-in-peril film, Marshall found that the American *The Cave* (Bruce Hunt, 2005), in which a group of cavers get offed by a band of killer troglodytes, not only had a remarkably similar plot but had also received the production green light. According to Marshall, *The Cave* began filming six months before he started filming *The Descent*, but he wanted to make a film that had more of a British sensibility about it, a form of bleakness that the American production would not have. As he said, "Let's get it out before them. That'll really piss on their chips" (qtd. in Clarke). The result was a fast-paced horror film of the first order.

After Sarah has gone whitewater rafting with her friends, she, her husband, Paul, and their daughter, Jessica, are involved in a car crash. Only Sarah survives. After a period of recuperation, during which she has a recurring nightmare about being trapped in a dark corridor, Sarah meets up with her friends to go on a caving expedition. Her uneasy friendship with Juno, who had an affair with Paul, is tested when she sends the group into an unknown cave system. As they go further into the depths, they begin to realize that there is a crawling horror waiting for them in the dark.

The gung-ho attitude of adventure-horror is right at the very heart of *The Descent*, arguably the outdoor film par excellence. Made over a short period of a few months on a budget of only £4 million and in postproduction right up until three weeks before its release, the film preys on three primordial fears within us all: being trapped underground, a fear of the dark, and a dread of something *in* the dark. Exterior location filming took place in Scotland. Neil Marshall felt that filming in a real cave system was too difficult and hazardous. Pinewood Studios became the location of the enormous cave sets built by the production team. To save time and money, each set could be bolted and unbolted into numerous shapes and configurations. This ingenious method of production is filmed so realistically that the film never feels studio bound.

Marshall originally wrote the film for a mixed-gender cast. However, his business partner felt that horror films almost *never* have a virtually all-female cast, so it was decided to make all the cavers women. Marshall didn't want them to be clichéd ladettes or victims. After getting advice from his female friends and colleagues, he tailored his story away from the gung-ho histrionics of the male troopers in *Dog Soldiers*, saying, "The women discuss how they feel about the situation, which the soldiers in *Dog Soldiers* would never have done" (qtd. in Clarke). He knew that he had to have credible, strong, but vulnerable characters. His chosen cast was solid, had an international flavor, and produced strong performances throughout, with Shauna MacDonald (Sarah), Natalie Mendoza (Juno), and Alex Reid (Beth) as the principal leads.

The Descent is a superior British horror film. The movie made over $58 million at the box office, which was indicative of its pull at playing on the audiences' fears of enclosure and monsters. This was not lost on the film's critics. *Time Out*'s Sarah Lilleyman called it "something truly disturbing." *Total Film* felt it was "tense, gory and masterfully malevolent" (*"Descent"*). Dan Jollin thought that the film was "brutal, bloody, terrifying, and so tense it'll leave you aching." Roger Ebert was stunned, comparing it to *Deliverance*, as "a savage and gripping piece of work that jangles your nerves without leaving your brain hanging. You emerge feeling energized and exhilarated rather than enervated or queasy" (*"Descent"*).

The movie works remarkably well on many levels. From a paranoia-induced feeling of claustrophobia when the cave crashes down around the cavers to the moral, physical, and psychological disintegration of its characters, Marshall's film remains arguably *the* most important British horror film of the twenty-first century so far.

Marshall wanted his female protagonists to be believable. All the characters are introduced quickly, with details sketched in early on. Even though some of the women are given the barest of backstories, each one remains significantly rounded enough for the audience to invest time, patience, and energy in actually getting to know them. They are treated realistically. When the women settle into the hut, they wear cozy, not sexy, pajamas. One of the women snores loudly. Another farts. Not once is the actresses' beauty directly foregrounded: they are women, they like caving, and they are physically and mentally strong. It makes them *believable*. Even the film's advertising campaign promoted the horror of the film, rather than the women's looks. One poster had them linked together to form a glowing skull, another saw Sarah in a blood-splattered portrait looking out at the audience, while the only sexualization of the characters is when a group portrait had the words "Take your pick" above them.

This believability definitely works in the film's favor. Due to the women's reasonably solid characterizations, their interaction with one another is convincing. This comes to the fore in two particular standout sequences. The first is when Sarah's backpack gets lodged on a rock, and with her now trapped and unable to move either forward or backward, her best friend, Beth, crawls back down the tunnel to get her. As the two face each other, with only about three or four inches of space around them, Beth tells Sarah to breathe slowly.

BETH: Breathe, okay? Hey, listen to me. What are you afraid of?
SARAH: Can't move. Can't breathe.
BETH: Sarah. Look at me. Look at me. Listen. The worst thing that could have happened to you has happened. You're still here. This is just a poxy cave, and there's nothing left to be afraid of. I promise. Okay? Okay! Listen to me. You'll love this one. How do you give a lemon an orgasm?
BOTH: Tickle its citrus.

They both laugh, and Beth gently prizes Sarah forward, taking her arm and slowly pulling her out of the gap.

BETH: Now. We're gonna move slowly. That's it. Grab my arm.

Okay. Slowly. Come on. Come on.

SARAH: The rope bag. It's stuck.

Sarah pulls on the bag. Suddenly the tunnel begins to collapse around them. The two of them remain still, the dust cascading over them. Beth looks up.

BETH: Right. Fuck the rope bag. Move! Come on! Move! Now!

Beth grabs Sarah and pulls her as she crawls backward down the tunnel. With the tunnel collapsing, dust flying all around, and the crawlspace getting narrower, the two women escape just before it is sealed behind them.

The scene's construction is simple: two shots and close-ups between the two women suggest camaraderie. The completely natural and humorous dialogue demonstrates Beth's caring side, while the last line emphasizes their situation *and* the closeness between the two. This physical and emotional closeness creates the overall power of this sequence. The skilled editing between the two women, who are lit only by their helmet lights, turns to feelings of claustrophobia, and the black edges of the screen encroach and surround not only them but also the audience. The final image of the women dragging themselves to freedom fades to black for five seconds, giving the audience time to catch their breath.

The second scene is after Beth tells Sarah that Juno stabbed her and left her to die at the Crawlers' hands. Sarah leads Juno through the caves, but the Crawlers attack them. The women kill the monsters by smashing their brains out on rocks, gouging out their eyes, and ramming summit axes into their skulls. As the women move onward toward the light and freedom, another set of Crawlers close in. Sarah stands in front of Juno, her axe raised ready to strike. Juno looks at her and then at Beth's pendant hanging from the weapon. Juno realizes that Sarah knows she left Beth behind and mumbles incoherently, but she is interrupted by the shouts of the Crawlers. Juno screams in agony as Sarah cuts her leg open with an axe. As Sarah moves toward freedom, Juno is left to fend off the oncoming Crawlers alone.

This sequence clearly demonstrates the fractured relationship between the two women. Sarah's life had been turned upside down more than once in the movie. The most blatant is the catastrophic descent into the caves. However, the most telling is *before* the car crash takes Paul's and Jessica's lives. Paul is emotionally distant and pulls away from Sarah as he looks at Juno. This is the catalyst for Sarah's mental fracturing. Therefore, over the course of a year spent in rehabilitation, where she has had time to think about her revenge on Juno, coupled with her knowing that Juno had abandoned Beth, the physical and emotional strain of Sarah's suffering becomes the silent, methodical rage that she metes out against Juno.

Sarah's journey and her disintegration into madness make the film take on an extra dimension of audience emotional attachment. Sarah has suffered. The car crash, the loss of her daughter's life, her haunted stay in the hospital, the tunnel collapse, her best friend dying, and then finally having to escape from the cave system have made her physically and mentally stronger. But her escape is short-lived. When she eventually breaks free from the caves, gulping, clawing, and gasping for air, she chances upon her car. She climbs inside and falls asleep. She wakes as a truck thunders past. As she turns, Juno's bloody face stares back at her. Suddenly Sarah wakes again. However, this time she is back in a small tunnel in the caves. Sarah turns and sees Jessica's birthday cake with lighted candles. Jessica sits in the cave opposite her. The camera moves back, and as the image of Sarah recedes into the distance, the sounds of the Crawlers gets nearer.

This ending, while sending the audience away with sufficient chills, makes the whole film come to this one single point. It pinpoints the moment when Sarah's own feral descent into madness becomes solidified. In a terrific close-up: her strikingly blue eyes pierce the blood that smothers her face. Her smile is not the smile of a mother loving her daughter but of a woman transformed into a Crawler. While audiences may have puzzled over the ambiguous ending, the clues to Sarah's mental breakdown are in evidence throughout the movie, forming a broken jigsaw puzzle of her fragile and emotional state that is slowly being put together again. When she is in the hospital, her recurring nightmare of being trapped in the corridor emphasizes that she is imprisoned within her own fractured and broken mind, where the hospital transforms into a metaphor for her fragile physical state. Perhaps Sarah has never actually left the hospital, and the whole film *after* the crash is really her own mind completely unraveling. That is up to the individual to decide.

Considering the film's low budget, Marshall and his production team have pulled off a coup. Working in virtual darkness, the film reminds the viewer of the work of Caravaggio, Fuseli's *The Nightmare* (1781), Goya's "black paintings" (notably *Saturn Devouring His Son*; 1819–23), and Dore's engravings for Dante's fourteenth-century *Inferno*. Each cave system the women enter, with the beams of helmet lights piercing the dark, damp recesses, not only reveals the chasm to the audience but simultaneously shrouds and creates more mysteries and horrors than at first glance. It is this approach that makes the film's visual style so strong. This visual sense of awe, wonder, and doom is linked to the earlier work of these artists and then cemented within the Gothic themes of anxiety and madness. The Crawlers' white and translucent skin, their sharply pointed feral teeth, and their blank-yet-staring eyes reflect the Gothic gargoyles of the twelfth and thirteenth centuries. While this link may be both subliminally and obviously made, the importance of those predecessors remains at the film's core. They give the film a genuine mythical quality of epic proportions. When coupled with Sarah's own descent into madness, the overall feel of the film becomes almost hallucinatory in its overall power and impact on both the characters, who *must* explore the caves, and the audience, who *must* keep watching them.

There are so many standout sequences in this film that demand attention. The women's first sight of the Crawlers through their night-vision cameras, the upside-down crawl over a gaping ravine, the collapsing tunnel, and the nightmarish scene of Sarah swimming through a lake of blood clearly reveal how good Marshall and his team were at creating such a brilliant atmosphere on a limited budget.

There is one scene that warrants attention for its use of color, size, scope, and meaning, and it is a pivotal moment in the narrative. When the cavers get their first view of the interior of the abyss, they become emblazoned in the bright red light of their flares. With this illumination comes a terrific sense of encroaching darkness, where the outcrops of jagged rocks, the layers of dust, and the whole vast cavern not only foreshadows their descent into hell but likewise plays psychological tricks with the audience. As the lights flicker and the shadows dance, the monsters appear and disappear around every corner. Or do they? The skills of cinematographer Sam McCurdy push the darkness into the distance, and the red vistas, the green filters of torches and camcorders, and the black spaces encroaching on the women become a vacuum where the real, the supposed, and the imaginary collide to grow into places of genuine horror for both characters and audience alike. This is why *The Descent* is such a remarkable, atmospheric, and disturbing horror film.

Throughout the analysis of these three modern British horror films, it becomes apparent that the great outdoors has provided filmmakers with terrific locations in which to place their horrors, and it has also helped them to bring inner meanings and subtexts to their narratives. *Severance* is not a simple siege movie. It takes pot shots at capitalism, office life, team bonding, and group dynamics. The final scene of Steve and Maggie escaping downriver is ambiguous at best. They may have survived the onslaught of the soldiers, and they may have become the strongest team members, but they also remain in the wilderness. For Jess in *Triangle*, the sea's undulating currents become the catalyst for her nightmares. It remains questionable whether she actually set sail on *Aeolus.* And

Sarah's physical and mental disintegration in *The Descent* is completed by her *becoming* a part of her location. Not only has she begun her physical transformation into one of the Crawlers that she has been so horrified by, but she remains trapped within the cave system, itself a metaphor for her own fragile state of mind.

This is what makes these films so important to the post-millennium's British horror genre. The great outdoors had always been used as a place of decay in the Gothic novels of yesteryear, and this followed into the world of film. Each of the films analyzed in this chapter reveals just how far modern British horror films have gone in using the geographical aspects of the landscape to help shape their narratives. It is true that American, European, and Asian horror had all done the same. However, even though *Severance*, *Triangle*, and *The Descent* may not have been set in Britain per se, there remains the overriding feeling that they are British. While Hammer's Gothic tales took the staple landscapes of a foreign locale and transformed them into backdrops through which their characters passed, films like the exciting *A Lonely Place to Die*, the gory *Wilderness*, and the brutal *The Seasoning House* used their locations as characters within their own right. This is so important to these rural horror films because the "human" characters become symbiotically linked to the areas in which they reside.

While the castle on the hill and the monsters in the wood may have had their origins in the fairy tales of Europe and the Gothic horrors of a bygone era, this new type of bucolic horror (far removed from such films as *Witchfinder General* and the like) utilizes the great outdoors in such vibrant and exciting ways that it has opened up the British countryside as a site of absolute terror rather than one with tourist trappings. These locales *look* real. They *smell* real. They *feel* real. They are not just backdrops to the narrative. They have become more than that. These locations have been used in such grim, grisly, and terrifying ways that they have impacted directly on the brittle mental states of their characters. This clearly shows that that location, location, location remains an important component of the modern British horror film.

3

THE DEAD INSIDE,
THE DEAD OUTSIDE,
THE STRANGER WITHIN

When David Pirie wrote that the British could lay claim to creating and owning their own staple cinematic genre, namely, the *horror* genre, he argued that the films of Hammer and others had been shaped by the remarkable popularity of the Gothic novels of the late eighteenth and nineteenth centuries (9). With tales of faraway castles, monsters striding across blasted heaths, ghostly apparitions, familial madness, and rotting corpses and a preoccupation with solitude and death among the ruins of the medieval world, Gothic writers like Horace Walpole, Charles Maturin, Ann Radcliffe, M. G. Lewis, Mary Shelley, Sheridan la Fanu, Bram Stoker, Charles Dickens, and the American Edgar Allan Poe lay the groundwork for astute filmmakers to fully exploit their own versions of oft-told tales.

During cinema's formative years, filmmakers used numerous Gothic chillers for inspiration. The tales of Faust and Mephistopheles, Maria Martin, *The Monkey's Paw*, *The Picture of Dorian Gray*, *The Ghost Train*, and *Sweeney Todd* all got numerous makeovers. These were usually low-budget and sensationalist trick films, in which macabre narratives were used to entice audiences into the theater. There were potboilers that focused on haunted houses, ghosts, ghouls and goblins, villainous schemers, dastardly villains, and homicidal maniacs, and a quick scout around the Internet reveals hundreds of lost "horror" films that—if found—would hopefully add an interesting cornerstone to cinema's love of the fantastique.

With the coming of sound, the British horror scene showed no sign of abating. Old favorites were wheeled out time after time to fairly muted success. As the war years took their toll, the horror film's decline was in evidence. However, after the conflict, filmmakers turned to horror once more. Movies like *The Queen of Spades* (Thorold Dickinson, 1948) stood out from the routine quota, but many of the old warhorses were trooped out yet again, with yet more remakes of *Uncle Silas* (Charles Frank, 1947), *The Monkey's Paw* (Norman Lee, 1948), and *Fall of the House of Usher* (Ivan Barnett, 1947) to entertain the crowds.

It was really only with the surprise success of Hammer's adaptation of Shelley's *Frankenstein: Or the Modern Prometheus* and Bram Stoker's *Dracula* that a recognizable "brand" of British horror was fully launched. Filmed in lurid Eastmancolor and boasting startling performances from Peter Cushing and Christopher Lee, both *The Curse of Frankenstein* and *Dracula* (Terence Fisher, 1958) were huge box-office hits. It was no surprise that Hammer, quickly followed by others, ramped up its productions for an eager, exploitation-seeking audience in Britain's postwar years. Their influence was far felt, and the "living dead" films of George A. Romero, the ghosts of John Carpenter, and the maniacal families of Tobe Hooper's productions all, at their heart, owe a massive debt of gratitude to Hammer's productions.

But whereas Hammer primarily focused on the traditional Gothic tropes, others tapped into Swinging Sixties and Dour Seventies zeitgeist, preferring to lens their films in the everyday. The past and the modern sat side by side with ease, and it was apparent that horror was now overtly beginning to question the very fabric of changes in British society itself. Films such as the psychedelic *The Sorcerers*, Hammer's Victorian-set *Taste the Blood of Dracula* (Peter Sasdy, 1969), and the cannibals-in-Britain romp of *Frightmare* may seem worlds apart, but their horrors were evident. On the one hand were the older generations preying on younger versions of themselves, while the teenagers were out to destroy their older counterparts. One thing remained constant. Every horror film *needed* a good monster.

These monsters may have been traditional vampires, zombies, or lumbering lycanthropes. However, one thing was apparent: as far as most audiences were concerned, the more frightening, violent, and grisly the better. There were all sorts of monsters to keep audiences entertained: manmade creations, ghosts, ghouls, goblins, demons, the devil, reptile women, cavemen, zombies, and even a snake-haired gorgon made an appearance. All were designed to thrill, scare, and terrorize, but they remained staid as creatures of ye olde world traditions, in which the savant comes riding over the hill to save the day. British horrors of the twenty-first century may rely on the hoodie rather than the slowly shuffling zombie, but they still remain reliant on using monsters in their narratives. It is to three particular types of monster that this chapter now turns.

THE DEAD INSIDE

The great British ghost story had its origins primarily in the literature of the Victorians. It was not hard to see why. Although Shakespeare's *Hamlet* used the ghostly figure of the dead king as a portent of impending doom, the great Gothic writers of the eighteenth and early nineteenth centuries had laid the foundations in their tales of the phantasmagorical. Horace Walpole's *The Castle of Otranto* (1764) had its fair share of haunted spirits, while in M. G. Lewis's *The Monk*, a whole portion of the book was devoted to telling the tale of a knight haunted by a spectral visitor.

It was not long before writers—in turn aided by the rise of the periodical press, the fascination with the burgeoning new technology of trick photography, and the investigations of the Society for Psychical Research into the macabre world of the séance, the medium, and the calling of the (un)dead—churned out short-form ghost stories for an often-undiscerning audience. Audiences lapped up these short tales, which were usually stuffed to the hilt with spectral hauntings, visitations, and other ghostly apparitions.

The best ghost stories are those in which the phantom is a malevolent spirit, hell-bent on tormenting its victims without any real discernible reason. There is no need to internalize the ghost. Rather, the ghost was there simply to frighten. Many of the earlier ghost stories were written in the foundations of the Gothic novel, but as time marched on, writers such as Sheridan le Fanu (1814–73), whose vampiric *Carmilla* (1871) predated Bram Stoker's

Dracula by twenty-six years, began to make way for a new style of ghost-story writer that kept one foot in the past while looking forward to the horrors of the late-Victorian and early-Edwardian eras. Henry James's (1843–1916) novella *The Turn of the Screw* appeared in *Collier's Weekly* in a serial format in 1898 and dealt with themes of repressed sexuality. Later writers like E. F. Benson (1867–1940), Algernon Blackwood (1869–1951), Alfred Noyes (1880–1958), H. R. Wakefield (1888–1964), and M. R. James (1862–1936) began to slowly move away from the "traditional" Gothic themes to create bolder, more frightening concepts that touched on antiquity, modernism, and horror with equally ghoulish delight.

With the advent of "trick films" such as *The Miser's Doom* (Walter R. Booth, 1899) and *The Haunted Curiosity Shop* (Walter R. Booth, 1901), huge crowds were drawn into theaters in search of more and more sensationalist entertainment. It was during the war years that a number of ghostly comedies made their appearance, and in many ways, these were designed to take an audience's mind off the real horrors of conflict. While a films like *The Ghost of St. Michael's* (Marcel Varnel, 1941) may have used Nazis as comic foils, it did have a purpose in alleviating the atrocities of war, if only for the briefest of times. The same could be said of *Old Mother Riley's Ghosts* (John Baxter, 1941) and *Blithe Spirit* (David Lean, 1945), which are at opposite ends of the ghostly cinematic spectrum. But all of these films used tried and tested comedic routines and cinematic sleight of hand to keep audiences entertained and their minds taken off the daily terrors that the country faced. As a riposte to these comedies, Ealing Studio's *Dead of Night* (Alberto Cavalcanti, Charles Chrichton, Robert Hamer, and Basil Dearden, 1945), with its portmanteau structure, offered some suitably shivery tales of ghostly revenge to great acclaim.

With the move into the 1960s and 1970s, ghost-story films became more expansive. Both the immensely impressive *The Innocents* (Jack Clayton, 1961) and *The Haunting* (Robert Wise, 1963) used their widescreen canvases to great effect, while also tackling themes such as incest and female sexuality. The children's drama *The Amazing Mr. Blunden* (Lionel Jeffries, 1972), *The Legend of Hell House* (John Hough, 1973), and *Ghost Story* (Stephen Weeks, 1974) showed just how diverse the British ghost-story movie could be. However, times change, and by the 1980s and 1990s, most British ghost-story films such as *High Spirits* (Neil Jordan, 1988), *Truly Madly Deeply* (Anthony Minghella, 1990), and *Haunted* (Lewis Gilbert, 1995) found very little commercial success.

The best ghost stories were made for British television. The BBC's series *A Ghost Story for Christmas* provided ample frissons of terror in the cold winter months.

Other notable successes included *Omnibus's Whistle and I'll Come to You* (1968) and *Schalcken the Painter* (1979), while Nigel Kneale's *The Stone Tape* (1972) terrified a generation of viewers. The influence of these programs can be felt today: *Sea of Souls* (2004–7) and *Being Human* (2009–13) have proved that the public has some sort of inner need to watch ghost stories. Whether this is in keeping with the lack of, or indeed need for, spiritual inner peace is open to interpretation. Whatever the reason, these series remain incredibly popular. Away from drama, arguably the most important "modern" TV ghost story was the BBC's ninety-minute *Ghostwatch* (1992), a mockumentary/reality-horror film focusing on a supposed live, on-air investigation of a house in Northolt, Greater London. Filmed weeks in advance, the film prompted over thirty thousand telephone calls to the BBC in its first hour of transmission, with viewers adamantly proclaiming that the program was too frightening to watch. While *Ghostwatch* remains an impressive achievement, the long-running *Most Haunted* (2002–present), in which a group of easily startled people and "celebrities" stumble around a "haunted" location, reveals a link back to the charlatans of the Victorian era's séance scene.

It seems only obvious that the revival of the modern British horror film would turn to the ghost film for some of its inspiration. Movies like *An American Haunting*

(Courtney Solomon, 2005) were coproductions with strong budgets, good casts, and inventive advertising. Others felt British in the way they developed their themes: *Oculus* (Mike Flanagan, 2013) springs to mind here. *The Gathering* (Brian Gilbert, 2003) and *The Dark* (John Fawcett, 2005) used the parochial horrors of England and Wales for their scares. For many filmmakers, the idea of the supernatural was merely a hook on which to hang their terrors. Therefore, films like *Nine Lives* (Andrew Green, 2002), *Credo* (Toni Harman, 2008), *Stormhouse* (Dan Turner, 2011), and *The Curse of the Witching Tree* (James Crow, 2015) may *appear* to be ghost stories but merely use the spirit world as a means to an end.

However, some modern British ghost films *do* warrant attention: *The Unkindness of Ravens* (Lawrie Brewster, 2016) was marked out as one of *Bloody Disgusting*'s "10 Must-See Independent Horror Films of 2016" (Thurman), while *Puffball* (Nicolas Roeg, 2007) and *Under the Skin* (Jonathan Glazer, 2013) were well-made, intelligent ghost stories that unfortunately remained far too elegiac for most audiences demanding easy scares. The superior *The Awakening* (Nick Murphy, 2011) was a very well shot and cast (Rebecca Hall, Dominic West, Imelda Staunton) old-style ghost story, set in a remote school for orphans. The film's 1921 period trappings gave it a solid feel, and the movie proved of interest because the female protagonist is a published author intent on debunking the headmaster's theories of paranormal phenomena. The debut film of the director Axelle Carolyn, *Soulmate*, caused some controversy when submitted to the British Board of Film Classification, when shots of a suicide attempt by the female protagonist, Audrey, were deemed too real. The modern-day setting of Wales (the Brecon Beacons) certainly helped the film, with its spooky, hidden village representing Audrey's state of mind during her period of recuperation. Strong performances by Anna Walton and Tom Wisdom bolstered a traditional narrative, and despite the movie's obligatory shock-tactic ending, it remains a solid entry in the British ghost-story stakes. However, one retelling of a ghost story stands out among the others, in terms of both production design and box-office clout. That film is the superior *The Woman in Black*.

Susan Hill's chilling tale of ghostly revenge was first published in 1983. Set in the late-Victorian era, the work is written in the style of *The Turn of the Screw*. Hill's prose is terrifying through its use of simple suggestion, rather than gore and violence. The book was a huge success and was successfully transformed into a long-running stage play. It has been adapted for radio and a spectacularly frightening TV movie in 1989.

A young, disillusioned, and melancholic solicitor, Kipps, visits Eel Marsh House near the secluded, mysterious village of Crythin Gifford at the bequest of his employer to sort out the last will of a client, Jennet Humfrye. The villagers are wary of Kipps, and none of them will discuss the house or its former inhabitant. A local landowner, Sam Daily, takes Kipps to Eel Marsh House but states that that he won't go into the property, and he tells Kipps to be quick about his business. When Kipps enters and sets to work among Humfrye's papers, he quickly realizes that someone, or something, is in the house with him.

The film was produced by Hammer Films, and the astute distribution company employed James Watkins to direct it. Watkins cast the fresh-faced Daniel Radcliffe—basking in glory from his *Harry Potter* movies—as the young solicitor, Arthur Kipps. The always-reliable Ciaran Hinds plays Sam Daily. Janet McTeer is his wife, Elizabeth. Shaun Dooley makes a welcome appearance as the rhubarbing villager Fisher. Sophie Stuckey appears in flashback as Kipps's wife, Stella. Liz White is Humfrye, the Woman in Black.

Jane Goldman wrote the movie. She had already entered into the fantasy genre with her screenplays for *Stardust* (Matthew Vaughn, 2007), *Kick-Ass* (Matthew Vaughn, 2010), and *X-Men: First Class* (Matthew Vaughn, 2011). Although Goldman's screenplay differs in its interpretation of the book—especially by omitting or rearranging the order of events—the main ingredients of the ghost story remain intact: Eel House gets cut off from the village of Crythin Gifford, the fog swirls, the young solicitor is abandoned by his mentor, a rocking chair moves on its own accord, and the ghost, at first glimpsed in the distance, becomes all too frighteningly real for the hero.

Shooting took nine weeks. The crumbling village of Crythin Gifford was filmed in the pretty village of Grassington, in the Yorkshire dales. Bluebell Railway in East Sussex, the Colne Valley Railway in East Anglia, and the Tudor palace of Layer Marney Tower in Essex were retro-dressed to fit the Edwardian feel of the film. The main location, Eel Marsh House, was Cotterstock Hall, an unscary, lived-in residence. The production crew re-dressed the house to include bolted-on ivy, fake cobwebs, and overgrown hedges, and they wanted to have the house dominate Kipps from every angle, from both the inside and the outside. Eel Marsh House, like Hill House, Hell House, and the monstrous house of *The Amityville Horror* (Stuart Rosenberg, 1979) before it, remains the main character at the film's core, surveying, provoking, and containing all its terrible secrets within.

The film was a huge box-office success. With a budget of approximately $15 million, the film took a staggering $127 million at the box office, with a further $12 million in DVD/Blu-ray sales. Roger Ebert gave the film three stars. His review was mixed. On the one hand, he felt that while Radcliffe looked too young and did not have much gravitas as Kipps, the house was the real star of the movie and was a "masterpiece of production design, crumbling, forlorn" ("*Woman*"). Amy Biancolli wrote for the *San Francisco Chronicle* and felt that while the film broke no new ground in horror, "the old ground it breaks is good, wet muck [where] eerie bests graphic and atmospheric trumps bold." Robbie Collin of the *Daily Telegraph* praised Radcliffe's performance, calling it "clear-eyed, plausibly grown up." He also felt that Watkins "expertly uses shadows and empty spaces to create a percolating sense of dread, and he waits until the last possible moment before allowing his audience the catharsis of a shock." Perhaps the best praise he gave the film was when he told audiences, "Don't be reassured by the 12A certificate: there's barely a glimpse of anything scary in this film, but that's precisely what makes it so terrifying."

The Woman in Black is a terrific and terrifying ghost movie. Hill's work had already provided enough thrills and chills to satisfy the most demanding of readers and theater audiences, and so it seemed only natural that the newly reformed Hammer Films would use an audience's preexisting knowledge of the text to transform it into a shocker of its own. Although the film may not tap into the horror crowd that expected gore, shocks, and mayhem, Watkins's frisson-filled chiller, with its superb production design, strong cast, and excellent atmosphere, is a movie that will leave an audience suitably chilled.

Radcliffe gives a believable performance as the haunted Kipps. While Hammer had used him and his *Harry Potter* persona to get bigger bucks at the box office, his performance as Kipps, despite its difference from Hill's progenitor, breaks free from his past work. Whereas Hill's Kipps was a happily married man, full of enthusiasm for his role as soon-to-be parent, Radcliffe's interpretation is its complete antithesis. His wife has died in childbirth, and he sees his son as a constant reminder of bitter regret and resentment at the death of his wife. This changes the trajectory of the character completely. He should be a happy man intent on doing a good job who gets caught up in extraordinary events. However, from the film's outset, Kipps's haunted and melancholic figure clearly shows that he is a shell of a man trying to achieve a form of contentment by battling both his internal demons and the external ones of Eel Marsh House. This characterization works in the film's favor because Kipps's physical, mental, and metaphorical disintegration becomes more manifest each time he sees or feels the ghostly presence at the house. As he walks through the property, axe in one hand and a lighted candle in the other, there is no heroism here, only fear, fright, and a genuine sense of dread.

For a period horror film, believability is the key to creating a setting in which the actors can then create their roles and the director can fashion his or her scares. A film like *The Woman in Black* relies on its production design. The film's Edwardian period production design is stunning. The village and its mistrusting occupants may be a standard trope of the ghost story, but with its crumbling cottages piled high over one another, Crythin Gifford is completely realistic. Even the costume design of the villagers, with their damp shirts, patched-up trousers, and dirty neckties all add to the general feeling that the house pervades and destroys everything it overlooks.

Dominating the film is the stunning Eel Marsh House, itself a masterpiece of production design. All the best ghost-story movies have, at their core, a location in which the ghost roams and the hero takes flight. From the first dominating shot of the house towering over the landscape, it haunts. It stares. It destroys. Here lies the masterstroke of the design team. Everything at Eel House is of significance. From the tiniest details to the largest props, the film's overall haunting tones are picked out in the design of this crumbling edifice. Staircases, doors, tables, lampshades, bookcases, bedside ottomans, blankets, sheets, books . . . *everything* has been designed to create an over-all ambience of melancholic dread to Eel House. The atmosphere is predictably dark, and candlelight has been maximized to create flickering shadows. The mist outside, handprints on the windows, original vintage artifacts (including dead-eyed porcelain dolls, stuffed animals in glass boxes, family portraits with eyes scratched out, and bizarre, spooky children's toys) are given extra shudders because the color palettes of grays and sepias make the film so *believable*. For Kipps, it is this believability that becomes his undoing. For the audience, the house may be viewed as clichéd, but its importance to the narrative *and* the film's atmosphere cannot be underestimated.

The main aspect of *The Woman in Black* is that it has to be frightening. As with all good ghost stories, there are the regular numbers of jump shocks for the audience. How-ever, the real strength of the film lies in what *may* be seen at the corners of each frame. Every scene suggests that something is lurking, ready to pounce out at Kipps. There are scenes in which the buildup of suspense is almost unbearable, and there are no cathartic shock payoffs for the viewer. This growing feeling of tension and anxiety builds further as Kipps moves into the shadows of the house, and when he stands close to frame, the most subtle shadows reveal Humfrye standing behind him. While the full appearance of the Woman in Black is suitably horrid, it is through the sparing use of the ghost being glimpsed that not only impacts on the characters and the audience but makes this terrific ghost story so frightening.

THE DEAD OUTSIDE

"Zombie!" shouts Sir James Forbes as he pushes away his protégé, Dr. Peter Thompson, from the slowly shambling, green-tinged, rotting corpses of Hammer Films' remarkable *The Plague of the Zombies*. Set in a small fishing village in Victorian Cornwall, the local squire, fresh from his trip to the West Indies, has concocted an army of the living dead to work in his tin mines. Only Sir James, a retired physician visiting his friend Peter can save the day and return the undead back to their proper resting places. Quite. However, despite the film's barmy story line, its sequence of the living dead rising from their graves, with its tilted camerawork, green-tinged imagery, deliberately paced editing, slowly pulsating music score, and genuinely frightening monsters, remains as chilling, mesmeric, and as influential as it ever did.

The first zombie movie was *White Zombie* (Victor Halperin, 1932), a routine low-budget horror flick starring Bela Lugosi. The later film *The Ghost Breakers* (George Marshall, 1940) treated its zombies as comedic stooges, but *I Walked with a Zombie* (Jacques Tourneur, 1943), a version of *Jane Eyre* set in the sweltering heat of the tropics, was suitably creepy. Most zombie movies, including *Revenge of the Zombies* (Steve Sekely, 1943), *Zombies of Mora Tau* (Edward L. Cahn, 1957), and *Teenage Zombies* (Jerry Warren, 1959), used the shambling undead as background threats amid the low budgets, falling scenery, and teenybopper shenanigans.

Today, the most famous of all things zombie remains American. The nightmarish *The Night of the Living Dead* may have been inspired by *Plague of the Zombies*, but it certainly overtook the earlier film as the most influential of the "modern-day" zombie films, with Romero churning out five bona fide sequels and the film spawning numerous remakes and spectacularly grim and grisly Italian exploitation horror versions.

However, while Romero's legion of the dead shambled around Pennsylvania, the British zombie had a quieter time. There were zombie rumblings in *The Woman Eater* (Charles Saunders, 1958), *Doctor Blood's Coffin* (Sidney J. Furie, 1961), and *The Earth Dies Screaming* (Terence Fisher, 1964). The 1970s saw the living dead pop up in *Tales from the Crypt* (Freddie Francis, 1971) and *Horror Express* (Eugenio Martin, 1972), while the delirious double whammy of *Psychomania* (Don Sharp, 1972) and *Horror Hospital* (Anthony Balch, 1973) used Hells Angels and mummified corpses to flesh out their already-convoluted narratives. But these zombies weren't the real deal. They were "added attractions." It was only with the remarkable *The Living Dead at the Manchester Morgue* (Jorge Grau, 1974) that the British zombie film truly came of age and offered a genuine challenge to Romero's groundbreaking film.

It was with the release of *28 Days Later* (Danny Boyle, 2002) that zombies were brought back to undead life in spectacular fashion and out into the mainstream. With a budget of $8 million, the film made over $84 million at the box office, proving that a contextually relevant theme (in this case, animal testing and cruelty) could find success on the international stage. The postapocalyptic thriller showed the breakdown and collapse of a British society following the release of a highly contagious toxin that turned the individual into a fast-moving, rage-filled zombie. The opening sequence of a desolate and deserted London is a remarkable piece of filmmaking, based primarily on the first twenty minutes of the BBC's adaptation of *The Day of the Triffids* (1981). As the hero, Jim, wakes in his hospital bed and spends the next twenty minutes wandering alone around the familiar tourist sites of Big Ben, the Houses of Parliament, and Trafalgar Square, the isolation he feels becomes so disorienting for the audience that the rest of the movie seems like an anticlimax. When he meets up with other survivors and heads for the apparent safety of the North, only to be met with violence at the hands of a group of soldiers, the film slowly descends into psychobabble and boring drivel. Despite the film's bleak but faintly optimistic ending, it took the far superior sequel, *28 Weeks Later* (Juan Carlos Fresnadillo, 2007), to really fashion a zombie movie that successfully combined the local, national, and international global threat of the virus to genuinely devastating effect.

Such was the success of *28 Days Later* and the fast-paced zombie flick *Resident Evil* (Paul W. S. Anderson, 2002) that the gory, funny, homespun, sitcom-like movie *Shaun of the Dead* was released to surprisingly rave reviews upon its release. The film stars Simon Pegg and Nick Frost as two likable friends (Shaun and Ed) who are obsessed with playing video games and spend most of their waking hours in their local pub, the Winchester Arms. When the country goes into shutdown following a zombie outbreak, they rescue Shaun's mother, girlfriend, and her friends and barricade themselves into the pub, hoping to stave off the zombie threat.

The film, derived from an episode of Pegg's Channel 4 program *Spaced* (1999–2001), pays homage to Romero's films, Sam Raimi's *Evil Dead* trilogy, and countless other popular-culture film and TV programs. The film works best as a comment on the slacker generation of the early twenty-first century, focusing as it does on the humdrum, everyday existence that the majority of people endure in the faint hope that their lives will end happily ever after. The opening sequence of Shaun walking to a corner shop and then catching the bus to work highlights just how somnambulistic everyone has become. People shuffle in bus queues, they walk slowly down the street, and the regulars at the pub stare into their drinks. This is zombiedom *but for the living*. This is what makes *Shaun of the Dead* so fascinating in the way that it reflected British daily life in such a depressing way. That it did so with such cheeky verve proved the point that horror films do mirror the world in which they are created.

Other zombie films quickly followed. *The Abandoned* (Nacho Cerda, 2006), *I Am Zombie Man* (Nick Thomson, 2007), *Battle of the Bone* (George Clarke, 2008), the £45-budget *Colin* (Marc Price, 2008), *The Dead* (Howard Ford and John Ford, 2010), *Zombie Woman of Satan* (Steve O'Brien, 2009), and the megabudget period horror *Pride, Prejudice and Zombies* (Burr Steers, 2016) were only a handful of the many zombie-themed films that were made.

However, one strain of zombie film boomed in the twenty-first century: Nazi zombies. This subgenre was certainly shocking but really nothing new. *The Frozen Dead* (Herbert J. Leder, 1966), *Shock Waves* (Ken Wiederhorn, 1977), *Zombie Lake* (Julian de Laserna and Jean

Rollin, 1980), *Oasis of the Zombies* (Jesus Franco, 1981), *The Bunker* (Rob Green, 2002), *Dead Snow* (Tommy Wirkola, 2009), and *Blood Creek* (Joel Schumacher, 2009) clearly confirmed that the exploitation field certainly knew how to tap into real horror beyond anyone's imagination. However, it was the film *Outpost* (Steve Barker, 2008) that proved to be the most interesting of all these (Nazi) zombie movies.

Although *Outpost* isn't strictly a zombie film, inasmuch as it doesn't feature the traditional living dead, it does have cadaverous-looking, slow-moving Nazi soldiers who have been reanimated some sixty years after they last saw battle. Arguably they are ghosts but ones that can shoot, stab, and kill just as easily as zombies can physically tear a body to pieces. That they do so with silence, their SS rifles, and bayonets makes them one of the odder entries into zombie filmdom.

The film's origins start in the work of the short-film producers Kieran Parker and Arabella Page Croft. Parker was developing a screenplay about modern-day troopers caught up in time-travel experiments, which results in them fighting soldiers from different time periods. After Parker showed his work to his friend Steve Barker, who was simultaneously developing a project for Parker and Croft's Black Camel Pictures, it was agreed that the theme of Nazi zombies was a tantalizing idea, and one that could be developed into a full-blown, though low-budgeted, project.

Rae Brunton was drafted in to hone and sharpen Parker and Barker's ideas into a workable script. He felt that with the collapse of the Cold War, the opening up of new frontiers that had been both hidden for such a long time and subjected to occupation, conflict, and oppression would serve as a strong backdrop to his plot. The story has a mysterious "Company" engineer desperately trying to find a hidden bunker in eastern Europe that may contain a secret Nazi superweapon. He hires a group of mercenaries to help him locate this concealed fortress. When the group eventually find it, they discover a labyrinth of underground corridors eventually leading to two rooms. In one is a pile of corpses stacked in the corner. As the soldiers approach, one of the bodies breathes. They take the man to a cellar and attempt to interrogate him. However, he remains mute and just stares at them. The second room houses the secret weapon. The engineer begins working on the machine, and eventually it sparks into life. He tells the soldiers that the machine represented the Nazis' last attempt to win the war. By using Einstein's unified field theory, they were trying to create a race of indestructible supersoldiers to end the war in one decisive military campaign. Unknown to the engineer and the soldiers, the machine's revitalized calibrations have brought back from the fourth dimension a squadron of SS troops, originally sent there to destroy the machine in 1945.

When the script, mood board, and poster were shown at the Cannes Film Festival, the film became a bit of a cause célèbre. Whereas Parker had taken a bold step in remortgaging his home to raise the projected £200,000 budget, both he and Croft found that the film was a hot property that was wanted by exhibitors and distributors intent on making a quick buck out of such an exploitative story line. When the film presold to thirteen international markets, the producers found that rather than filming in a small studio and on digital video, they could now afford thirty-five-millimeter film stock, have better production values, pay renowned actors, hire a bigger crew, and film both in a real film studio and on location.

Rather than being filmed in eastern Europe, the film's indoor sequences were shot on the sound stages at Film City Glasgow studios, while exteriors were filmed near the Scottish towns of Dumfries and Galloway. Shooting took place over four very cold weeks in January–February 2007. The photography is spectacular: scenes of the forest lit up at night, with the SS troopers striding through the trees, sends a genuine quiver of fright down the spine, just as much as the notion that the Nazis have returned to claim their prize does. Much of the crew had worked on

Barker's, Croft's, and Parker's previous projects, and production ran smoothly.

The cast was solid. The actor Ray Stevenson played the lead mercenary, DC, a British Royal Marine; the sepulchral-voiced Richard Coyle was Wallace; and the well-respected theater, TV, and film actor Julian Wadham played Hunt, the engineer. Brett Fancy, a noted theater and television character actor, played the Russian mercenary Taktarov. The genre favorite Michael Smiley—probably best known for playing the maniacal Tyres in *Spaced*—was the foul-mouthed opportunist McKay. For the role of the gaunt, expressionless Brigadeführer, Gotz, Johnny Meres made an ideal choice.

The film debuted in America on 11 March 2008 and in the United Kingdom on 16 May 2008. Reviews for the film were mixed. Anton Bitel of *Eye for Film* felt that the film was not wholly original but conceded that it was both "insidious and atmospheric" while being "a slick, stylish genre piece that gallops along and grips from its no-nonsense beginning to its bleakest of endings" (*"Outpost"*). Pvt.Caboose91 gave the film eight out of ten on *Manly Movie* and thought that the cinematographer, Gavin Struthers, captured the film's atmosphere superbly. Because of the cinematography, coupled with Barker's direction, the reviewer felt that despite a lack of any character development, the overall effect of the film was a "damn solid chiller and a worthy picture to behold in an age of torture porn, horror remakes and hackneyed slasher pictures." *Rue Morgue*'s Dave Alexander didn't think the film was a classic horror film but was prepared to say that it was "relentlessly tense with more than a few chilling moments and well-executed jump scares that make the most of the film's shadowy, airless setting." Philip French, reviewing for the *Observer*, thought it was "derivative, mediocre, yet watchable." David Nusair's *Reel Film Reviews* criticism was leveled mostly at the director, and he felt that the first hour could easily have been compressed into a "tightly-wound 15-minute chunk" that would have developed more for their characters than the original hour had. Perhaps Tristan Wright hit the nail on the head regarding the mood and aims of the film when he said, "Never has the unveiling of a swastika ever felt so terrifying and exciting at the same time."

The film is an excellent entry in the modern British horror film canon. Without any hint of any tongue-in-cheek shenanigans, *Outpost* has attempted to create, and succeeded, a ghost/zombie narrative that remains both intriguing and unsettling even after several viewings. By setting the film in a post-*Glasnost* world, the film is both contextualized and grounded in a firm location, much as *Severance* had done with its eastern European settings. There are hints of people living wild in the woods, the mercenaries cannot find any means of escape, and the history of the location seems to contain a force of over-powering evil.

It is fitting that this zombie movie uses capitalism as part of its narrative themes, much in the same way that *Severance* did. In *Outpost*, Hunt works for an anonymous and sinister "Company," which could easily be Palisades from the earlier film, hinting at the idea that the evils of capitalism have once again reared their ugly head. Although this idea is not deliberately or blatantly linked to the themes of Nazism in the narrative, nor is there an attempt to make a contextual comment on the manufacturing of arms in the modern day, the inference is still there. The unified field theory generator may be a MacGuffin, a hook to lure the soldiers into the bunker and for audiences to enjoy, but it is very much like Palisades' arsenal of weapons, which is there to be sought after, taken, and then exploited.

With the bleakness of the surroundings closing in around the soldiers, the revealing of humankind's inhospitable nature becomes apparent. The landscape, with its twisted, gnarled trees, open terrain, and frozen ground, begins to encroach on the men. When sniper fire pins down the mercenaries at the entrance to the bunker, they can't see anyone to return fire at. After the shooting stops, Taktarov runs into the trees but finds no one. One of the team suggests that it is a passing patrol, while the others look on skeptically. Later, in the darkness, when the soldiers come under attack, they get picked off one by one by unknown assailants. As dawn breaks, the men find two of their comrades standing upright, facing each other, dead: they have been bolted together through their heads, with a flag tied around them.

When the SS troops make their first appearance, the overwhelming effect is startling. The unified field theory generator hums into life, its resonating sounds creating the vortex that brings the soldiers back from the fourth dimension. As the mercenaries run outside, they see the forest spectacularly lit up. Standing among the trees are the Nazi soldiers, silhouetted against the blinding light of the maelstrom behind them. The camera cuts from a wide shot of the zombies to a tilted medium close-up of Gotz. He takes one step into the light, and his features remain motionless, blank, and staring. This terrific sequence, in which light and shadow either reveal or hide the monsters, shows that as in films like *Severance*, *A Lonely Place to Die*, and others in the survivalist-horror subgenre, the terrain hides all manner of monsters.

Inside the bunker, the tunnels become a symbolic representation of the unraveling of the men's minds. As they retreat back into the bunker, each man is killed, and the tunnels get progressively darker, until only DC and Hunt are left standing. With the undead Nazi troopers slowly closing in, DC stands and fights: this is *British* heroism to the last. Hunt crawls through a network of pipes in the vain hope of escape. When he finally reaches his destination, Gotz stands ahead of him, flanked by his legion of the undead. Gotz's gaunt figure remains half in shadow, half in light. The zombies' features are completely obscured. For Hunt, there is no escape. As he stumbles backward down the tunnel, the troops slowly advance toward him. He moves in and out of light: the metaphor reveals that in light he can see the horrors of his creation and that the dark will soon become his undoing. It is the bleakness of this ending that comes to clearly demonstrate that even sixty years after the end of the war, the idea of Nazism, and in particular neo-Nazism and its rise back into the headlines of the twenty-first century, is still as foreboding, horrible, and horrifying as anything a filmmaker could conjure up. That is what makes *Outpost* so impressive.

THE STRANGER WITHIN

Despite all these undead monsters, there is one that remains at the heart of virtually every single horror film. *Us*. As discussed previously, humans' inhumanity to humans is all too apparent in these horror films. Hoodies standing on street corners, invading schools, terrorizing families, and roaming the streets like mindless animals; mad soldiers garroting sales representatives; broken-minded individuals reliving the same day time after time; nature-twisting cave monsters; vengeful spirits; time-traveling Nazis—all seem to represent humankind at its most horrid. And the modern British horror film revels in its celebration of these terrors.

Perhaps it is worthwhile briefly considering the destructive nature of humankind one more time through the eyes of the modern British horror film family. Monsters have always roamed the streets to prey on the young, the helpless, and the needy. The tabloid press, news channels, online outlets, and other sources of media information have all used these monsters to help divide an already-fractured cultural landscape. British society has always been fractured to some degree. In today's media-dominated climate, those divisions are multiplied a hundred times over, so that anything deemed Not Us is therefore a horror for British society. The follies of (now former) prime minister David Cameron's egotistical Brexit vote rebounded on him so spectacularly that he had no choice but to resign in shame, while the Brexiteers whooped with delight that Britain would no longer be part of a European community but rather will be *British*. Brexit certainly highlighted the divisions that have hidden under the cultural surface of a Britain mired in scaremongering tactics from the media for years. This once outward-looking country is becoming more and more insular, where the ideas of anything "foreign" are frowned on. There are daily stories of violence between "us" British and "those" foreigners, and the country could well—at the time of this writing—be taking a faltering step over the edge of the abyss and into a dismal era of a new Dark Age. When coupled with the explosive headlines of Operation Yewtree, which singled out celebrities and high-profile figures and their horrific sexual crimes, it seems as if the monsters are not hidden away in some Gothic castle. Rather, the real monsters are the people next door. Everyone, it seems, is capable of being a monster, and the modern British horror film is intent on capturing these fractures in British society with relish.

There are many films in the resurgent horror genre that warrant attention in the way that they deconstruct the horrible world of Britain in the twenty-first century. One of the most potent and challenging is undoubtedly *The Last Horror Movie* (Julian Richards, 2003). Max, a wedding photographer cum serial killer, films his atrocities, editing them together while talking to the camera as his confidant. This plotline demonstrates the power of filmmaking at its most raw. When the "real" world of the killer seeps out into the fictional world of the film but then becomes "real" because the audience watching it is real, the (fictional) insights into the mental collapse of an individual can begin to be deconstructed in such a way that the very nature of "viewing" is starting to be questioned.

Christopher Smith's claustrophobic *Creep* may seem a simple killer-on-the-loose stalk-'n'-slash movie set in the gloomy tunnels of the London underground, but when two characters are killed simply because they are living roughly and hiding in the network of passageways, the film becomes a discourse on the treatment of those who are on the periphery of British society. The same can be said of the tightly wound thriller *Hush* (Mark Tonderai, 2008), in which the immigrants and underclasses of both the Conservative- and Labour-government eras become the sexual and torture victims of gangs selling them to the highest bidders. Even the art-film horror film *Kill List* (Ben Wheatley, 2011), with its graphic visuals, can lay claim to making us question the very nature of horror, love, relationships, and the importance of violence in a violent world. These horror films begin to poke, prod, and dissect the very society that they belong to. With that in mind, there is one final movie that needs to be discussed that really gets to the root of the monster in the modern British horror film. That movie is the terrific *Mum & Dad* (Steven Sheil, 2008).

Produced under the "Microwave Scheme" of funding innovative, low-budget (less than £100,000) films and with a release funded in part by BBC Films, Steven Sheil's Nottingham-based *Mum & Dad* is a strong contender for the United Kingdom's most significant horror film of the twenty-first century. *The Texas Chainsaw Massacre, Frightmare*, and *Mumsy, Nanny, Sonny and Girly* influenced Sheil's filmmaking. He liked their raw and gritty styles and created a film that reflected their (and the original Gothic novels') story lines of familial madness, incest, and decay. He approached the Film London agency after it saw his short movie *Cry*, and he pitched his new project as making "The Heathrow Airport Chainsaw Massacre." They were hooked.

With a small budget of between £100,000 and £200,000 split between Film London and Em-Media and with a talented cast and crew at the ready, the film was shot over eighteen days in 2007. Despite the Heathrow Airport setting, filming took place in Nottingham. Interviews and behind-the-scenes footage on the DVD release capture the difficulties and ingenuities of working on a low production. Jess Alexander (production designer) discusses creating a house that looks real but is all on sound stages; Jonathan Blook (director of photography) demonstrates his attempts at creating a sordid visual atmosphere; and the special-effects crew gleefully demonstrate their skills at getting blood to both ooze and congeal with equal ease, which all prove an interesting insight into the difficulties of getting films funded, even through initiatives and low budgeting.

The film premiered at FrightFest, 8 August 2008. It was the first British film to receive a multiplatform release, and hopes for the movie were high. On 26 December 2008, it got a cinema release over eleven screens and was released on DVD, through VOD (via Sky Box Office and FilmFlex), and also as a download through LoveFilm and Blinkbox.

In the film, a young Polish immigrant, Lena (Olga Fedori), works at Heathrow Airport as a shift cleaner. She misses her last bus home but accepts an invitation by her coworker Birdy and her mute brother, Elbie, to go back to their parents' house for the evening. Once there, Mum and Dad begin to torment Lena. They drug her, chain her to a filthy bed, and force her to work in their cellar separating and cleaning clothes that Dad has stolen from his shift work as a baggage handler at the airport. Lena eventually attempts an escape, but only after enduring a Christmas Day when Dad sexually threatens her while a crucified corpse drips blood and guts onto the lounge carpet.

The reception of the film was mixed. Scott Macdonald felt that the film was a satirical and "savage deconstruction of Thatcherite beliefs in Britain" and that "simple authenticity lends credence to the belief that these savage murderers live amongst us." Jeremy Heilman thought that the film was a "full-on assault against the family unit." Leslie Felperin felt that these *British* extremes were pallid compared to the grotesqueries of the American *Saw* (James Wan, 2004) and *Hostel* (Eli Roth, 2005). Despite acknowledging that the film had a truly chilling atmosphere that was enhanced by the gloomy cinematography and strong performances, she wrote that it was "too silly to be properly scary." However, Matthew Turner felt that the script wasn't at all silly. He considered its black humor to work in its favor. He praised the cast as being uniformly excellent and said that the film was "an entertaining, uniquely British horror flick" that was "chilling, squirm-inducing and darkly funny."

Traditionally, the family unit is seen as the bedrock of society. However, David Cooper's book *The Death of the Family* (1971) examined the idea that the "family" as a unit of love, care, warmth, and support was nothing of the sort. In the post-Manson-massacre years, American movies such as *Let's Scare Jessica to Death* (John Hancock, 1971), *The Last House on the Left* (Sean S. Cunningham, 1972), and *The Texas Chainsaw Massacre* (Tobe Hooper, 1974) or the British *Beast in the Cellar* (James Kelly, 1971) and *Death Line* (Gary Sherman, 1972) showed the family unit to be both corrosive and destructive. This was nothing new. The Gothic literature of the past had families in which the members constantly preyed on one another.

Cooper felt that the "family" held people back, clinging to the family as a limpet clings to a rock. The family was not wholesome at all, and therefore due to this destructive element, traditional "family values" were breaking down. Although *Mum & Dad*'s "traditional" parents are anything but conventional, in their defense, they attempt to provide a loving and caring environment, where their children are shown a conservative moral responsibility to get jobs, to provide for the others, and to show respect to their parents. That they do this through an atmosphere of terror and violence shows the flipside to this idea. The older generation acknowledges its own role within the family sphere, where Dad provides food and shelter, Mum looks after the household, and the children "do as they are told."

Sheil's approach to filming his subject matter is intriguing. Filmically, the movie is strong: the narrative begins at Heathrow, where cleaners begin their night shift. Lena and Birdie strike up a conversation as they clean a toilet smothered in feces. This is done through low, blue lighting, which reflects the sterility of the area. However, while the family's residence at the end of the runway looks normal and the kitchen is spotless, the rest of the dwelling resembles nothing more than a charnel house. Here the color scheme moves away from sterile blues to grotesque browns and reds that emphasize dirt, grime, blood, excrement, and sex. Sheil's treatment of the family is also interesting. Birdie and Elbie are not related but have a strangely concocted sense of sibling rivalry. Birdie constantly whines to her "parents" that she is their number-one child, while Elbie remains mute. The parents' relationship with each other is based on patriarchal lines, where Mum is almost always in control of her emotions, whereas Dad is constantly ranting and raging at the slightest upset. When Dad complains about the "kids" making a noise, he screams, "I just want to read my fucking newspaper in fucking peace and quiet!" which may speak volumes to many fathers up and down the land.

Where the film really begins to deconstruct the notion of "family" is through its brutal depictions of violence, the threat of sexual violence, and the breakdown of traditional family life. Dad masturbates into a slab of meat, a crucified man's stomach is slit open, and Mum gently caresses and strokes Lena before injecting her with poison—scenes that are there for the audience's delectation. But they also begin to question the audience's tastes for this movie: are they really enjoying what they are being presented with, or is the movie questioning their own approach to ideas about familial life and responsibilities?

Sheil does attempt to answer these questions. By clearly showing how corrupting the parents are, he puts the audience into a position of identifying with Lena. Dad's behavior is both constantly threatening and sickening. Mum's dominance, whereby she is simultaneously suckling provider and vicious harridan, ensures that Lena and the audience are constantly put on edge. This dynamic is made apparent in two standout sequences. The first is when Lena tries to grab the attention of one of Dad's friends and colleagues from the airport. As she sorts through clothes in the washroom overlooking the garden, she finds a set of teeth with the mouth's palate still attached. She realizes that this is the only thing small enough that she can throw out the window to attract the man's attention. However, Elbie walks in, and Lena quickly puts the teeth in her own mouth to hide them. After Elbie leaves, Lena throws the teeth out to the man, but Dad finds them and goes back into the house to beat her. He then returns outside to kill the man. Later that day, as they all sit around the kitchen table eating a roast dinner, Elbie walks in with a plastic bag in his hand. In it are the man's intestines, stomach, and liver. Mum places them in a mincer and turns them into sausages.

The second sequence takes place on (possibly) Christmas Day. As the Yuletide festivities begin, Dad brings down Angela, his brain-dead *real* daughter from the attic. Elbie props her up in a chair. Above the mantelpiece is the body of the crucified man, a candle lit and placed in his stomach. As presents are handed around, Dad swigs from a bottle of brandy. He looks at Lena and begins to fondle her. Later, when she is alone in her room, Dad walks in. He pulls down his trousers and says, "Look what I've got for you. Be a good girl. You just lie there." He moves toward her, but she stabs him repeatedly in his back. With Dad lying motionless on the bedroom floor, Lena begins to move furtively downstairs, while the traditional Christmas carol "God Rest Ye Merry Gentlemen" plays on the soundtrack.

These two scenes are important in deconstructing the family as keepers of a moral flame. Mum and Dad are opportunistic cannibals that feed on the scraps of humanity. In this case, it is hinted that these tasty morsels are all immigrants or Dad's best friend of fifteen years. No one is safe anymore. The family is as destructive as the *Other* and actually becomes the *Other* during the narrative. Therefore, the family unit does not form the bedrock of society but rather undermines it.

As this destabilization takes place, the relevance of the family being cannibals becomes evident. *This* family represents the potential within *all* families to seek self-preservation through any (capitalist and entrepreneurial) ways possible. The second scene just described clearly shows the cracks within the family unit. Angela, Dad's *real* daughter, is the product of his having sex with someone who is *not* Mum. Presumably she is the offspring of Dad raping another victim. Mum looks on disgusted when he says that Angela was "ripped from her mother" and that Dad tasted blood for the first time when he bit through the umbilical cord. The whole scene plays out as a cynical parody of the "typical" British Christmas Day celebrations. For the normal family, presents are given and turkey is eaten. For Mum and Dad, their presents are stolen, and everyone gorges on human flesh. Such is the power of these two sequences that while they may bear more than a passing resemblance to the similar family mealtime in *The Texas Chainsaw Massacre*, they make the audience acutely aware that the traditional family unit is now society's most destructive element.

The cast is uniformly excellent. Olga Fedori's performance gives both an inner strength and a vulnerability to Lena. Dido Miles's Mum is both chillingly kind and unswervingly perverse. As the mute son Elbie, Toby Alexander uses just his facial expressions to convey anger, fright, and eventual calmness as he strangles his adopted "sister." Ainsley Howard, in her first role, is pitch perfect as the scheming, violent, capricious, childish "daughter" who brings people back to the house and their doom. Already known to many viewers through roles in the films *Scum* (Alan Clarke, 1979), *Quadrophenia* (Franc Roddam, 1979), and *This Is England* (Shane Meadows, 2006) and the TV comedies *Hi de Hi!* (1980–88), *You Rang, M'Lord?*

(1988–93), and *Oh, Doctor Beeching!* (1995–97), Perry Benson is genuinely frightening as Dad. His change from smarmy kindness to violence and madness remains a tour de force in the modern British horror canon.

This tour de force approach remains chillingly bleak and pessimistic at the film's climax. After Lena has endured capture, torture, mental cruelty, beatings, and attempted rape, her first cries of freedom after she has hacked and stabbed at Dad are nothing of the sort. Running out into the blazing sunshine, Lena looks skyward, her screams turning to howls of anguish, hatred, fright, and relief. The last shot of the movie, with Lena overshadowed by a passing aircraft, is a truly haunting one. As the noise of the jet engines drowns out her screams, and traffic passes her by without even noticing her, the film's meaning becomes palpable. *Nothing* and *nobody* can help Lena. She may have survived, but her body and mind are destroyed. *This* becomes the point of *Mum & Dad.* The family unit, once the bedrock of society, has completely collapsed, revealing a hideous underbelly where nothing and no one is free or safe from danger.

CONCLUSION

The best horror films are undoubtedly those that not only frighten but also in some ways begin to question the very fabric of the society that has produced them. Carlos Clarens argued that the very best horror films become redolent with the meanings of their era. That might seem rather far-fetched or maybe one step too far removed from reality to be true. After all, horror films are there simply to frighten and to shock their audiences. Aren't they?

The answer to that question is "No!" The very best horrors, those that do not shirk from producing feelings of dread, fear, and terror, however subtle or unsubtle they may be, are those that *do* begin to pick apart and critique the contextual era in which they were made. Johnny Walker provides evidence that over five hundred horror films were registered, made, and released between 2000 and 2014. This is an incredible achievement and shows just how potent, important, and vital horror is to British cinema. While the mainstream cinematic view of Britain appears to be represented through heritage romps, middle-class comedies, or realist dramas, the horror film clearly indicates that Britain has more to offer than these clichéd views. Walker goes on to convincingly argue that modern British horror films are at the vanguard of a new style of filmmaking, in which elements such as burgeoning technology, intertextual revelry, and sophisticated social comment begin to offer a genuine chance to propel horror out of its dark, dank grave once and for all. I would go even further.

The horror films that Britain has produced since the turn of the millennium do not just deal with deconstructing a society that has become arguably more and more fractured through years of political unease, lack of genuinely engaging leadership, and a perceived collapse (at least from a right-wing media viewpoint) in morality. The *best* and the *worst* of British horror cinema seem to be harking back to the French ideas of fin de siècle, which clearly marks the closing of one era and defines the opening of another. For the horror film, this has meant that the older movies belonged very much in the past: *of their time.* But for the postmillennium horrors, the ennui, cynicism, and pessimism so redolent in British culture has now become the very food on which British horror films feast.

At the beginning of this book, I argued that *the* name most synonymous with British horror was Hammer Film Productions. It is not hard to see why. This small, independent production unit tapped into the zeitgeist of the time, when Britain was finding its power on the world's stage diminishing. The company's Gothic outings were originally seen as horrifying, but now they are quite clearly relics of a bygone era and very much reflected the social and cultural climate of their times. That remains a main point of horror cinema. Not only do the films provide nightmares for their audience, but they reflect the real terrors of the world back at them. Even though Hammer Films was revived in the twenty-first century, it still remains somehow linked to its past heritage. However, other filmmakers, both mainstream and independent, modernized and propelled the British horror film back into the limelight. This modernization may have played on the riffs of past directors like Michael Reeves, Pete Walker, and many others, but it also had to contend with the bigger budgets, increased production values, wider exhibition systems, and better distribution systems of Hollywood. It also had to stave off the graphic shocks of Japanese horror.

That the modern British horror film tackled Hollywood while staving off the graphic shocks of Japanese horror with vim and verve and with a feeling of both genuine excitement and engagement is a testament to the people who *believe* in the horror film as a means of understanding the world around them. Indeed, it could be legitimately argued that even though the British horror film of the twenty-first century focuses primarily on

Britain, it does have a major part to play alongside such other international horrors from Asia, Europe, and America in reflecting and commenting on the real-life horrors of a postmillennial world. While those movies certainly do hark back to the traditional ghost stories of the past, they do so with a playfulness that makes them all the more frightening. In Europe, the urban and rural horrors that have sprung up show a continent that is beginning to fracture under the strains of multicultural living. Yet it is obvious that all of these cultural constructs can survive together. This is where the British horror film can flourish as part of something *bigger*.

Horror films do not have to have huge budgets to create their terrors. A good script, strong acting, and atmosphere can all combine to produce diverse, spine-chilling films like *The Descent, Heartless,* and *Mum & Dad* that remain quintessentially *British* in both style and outlook. Their success is also testament to the viewer who has embraced the British horror movie so passionately. Although many of these horror movies would never see the light of day in a multiplex cinema, they are sought out by those who are eager to consume films they want to watch. This has worked in numerous ways. Bigger horror film festivals such as London's FrightFest, with its multiscreen options, big guest-star names, and corporate-style production glitz, sits easily alongside smaller, intimate ones such as

Abertoir in the wilds of West Wales, where the growing fan base meets up on or around Halloween every year to watch an eclectic mix of old, new, odd, bold, experimental, mainstream, and independent horror films. For the horror aficionado, fanzines such as *Dark Side Magazine* effectively combine nostalgia and modern horror together, while *Rue Morgue*, *Fangoria*, and others take a more visceral approach to the genre, as their covers proudly display the latest gorefest for the delectation of their readers. And then there are the horror conventions, where thousands of fans attend in their homemade costumes, where *they* become the killer who dances the night away with like-minded people. And all this is marvelous.

In concluding this introduction to the modern British horror film, it becomes apparent that the Gothic wonders of yesteryear, those works that celebrated corporeal death, decay, familial incest, monsters in the fog, castles on the hill, and decrepitude at every corner, have altered (not too significantly) into the horrors of today. This was done in distinct ways, as seen in the chapters in this book. The hooded terror, the great outdoors, and the dead inside, outside, and within have, it is hoped, demonstrated how vibrant, challenging, and questioning the modern British horror film can be. The complexities and terrors of *Eden Lake* and others in the hoodie horror subgenre chew away at a media-dominated fixation and demonization of the hoodie. The capitalist-bashing *Severance*, the collapse of human existence in *The Descent*, and the disintegration of the human mind in *Triangle* offer both tangible and oblique questions about the human "condition." This "condition" is further deconstructed through a film like *Mum & Dad*, in which the bedrock of society is really its own undoing.

At the time of this writing, only seventeen years of the twenty-first century have elapsed. Yet in that time, an astonishing five-hundred-plus British horror movies have been made. Many will never see the light of day in the "traditional" sense of a cinematic release. The vast majority of them will be made available via streaming, downloading, ripping, subscribing, and numerous other methods, rather than a trip to the local cinema. The rise of the horror-film festival is something that *celebrates* horror in every sense of the word, as individuals come and share their ideas and watch the latest horror flicks. The technological means to view films in the cinema, at home, or on the way to work provide an ideal opportunity for the modern British horror film to survive and flourish even more than it has done.

Of course, all genres are cyclical by nature. They ebb and flow in and out of favor. Therefore, there is every chance that audiences may become bored of watching these horror films. However, as Walker suggests, the fact that the horror genre *has* survived and flourished is testament to its place in the overall pantheon of cinema (135–39). Horror films *should* be studied, and it does not matter if they are mainstream, independent, high-budget, low-budget, or zero-budget productions. What matters is that amateur, semipro, and professional filmmakers have the necessary tools at their disposal to make horror films quickly and efficiently for an audience that once upon a time may have been considered fan-boyish, nerdy, and geeky but is now regarded as an intelligent, motivated, driven fan base that celebrates ideas of horror as a *culture* within its own right.

The modern British horror film is replete with imaginative storytelling, strong acting, and great atmosphere. The multimedia platforms available to everyone offer a terrific chance for filmmakers to create horror films that probe and poke and prod at the very fundamentals of a British society undergoing social change and possible collapse. The subjects that can be covered are diverse. Traditional Gothic tropes remain in evidence, where the castle on the hill becomes the high-rise under siege. What the modern British horror film does best, though, is this: it *reflects* back to the viewer a society undergoing massive social change. Brexit, NHS cutbacks, immigration—these are areas of culturally contextual relevance that could well become the food for both current and future horror films.

Tap into them, reflect them, and critique them—that will provide both impetus and ideas for the modern British horror film for years to come.

Therefore, while monsters, ghosts, zombies, ghouls, hooded terrors, werewolves, and denizens from other worlds may stalk our streets or haunt our minds, the *real* horrors of today remain closer to home than maybe they should. Perhaps the ultimate monsters in the *great* modern British horror film don't stalk the castle on the hill but the streets where we live. Maybe they aren't the monsters created through lightning and science. Perhaps the *real* monsters of the modern British horror film aren't really the monsters out there at all. They are the monsters in here. *With us.*

ACKNOWLEDGMENTS

This book would not have been possible without the help and guidance of the following people: Wheeler Winston Dixon, Leslie Mitchner, Gwendolyn Audrey Foster, and Andrew Katz for their patience; Dr. Johnny Walker for advice and guidance; and, finally, Professor Robert Shail for suggesting my name be attached to this project in the first place. He has been a guiding source of inspiration, friendship, and cheap, fizzy lager for many a long year.

FURTHER READING

Cherry, Brigid. *Horror*. London: Routledge, 2009.

Chibnall, Steve, and Julian Petley. *British Horror Cinema*. London: Routledge, 2002.

Fahy, Thomas, ed. *The Philosophy of Horror*. Lexington: UP of Kentucky, 2010.

Forshaw, Barry. *British Gothic Cinema*. Basingstoke, UK: Palgrave Macmillan, 2013.

Frank, Alan G. *Horror Movies*. London: Octopus, 1974.

Gifford, Dennis. *A Pictorial History of the Horror Movies*. London: Hamlyn, 1973.

Hardy, Phil. *The Encyclopedia of Horror Movies*. London: HarperCollins, 1986.

Hills, Matt. *The Pleasures of Horror*. London: Continuum, 2005.

Jones, Steve. *Torture Porn: Popular Horror of the Era*. London: Palgrave, 2013.

Meikle, Dennis. *A History of Horrors: The Rise and Fall of the House of Hammer*. Rev. ed. Lanham, MD: Scarecrow 2009.

Pirie, David. *A New Heritage of Horror: The Gothic English Cinema*. London: I. B. Tauris, 2008.

Rigby, Jonathan. *English Gothic: A Century of Horror Cinema*. London: Reynolds and Hearn, 2006.

Rigby, Jonathan. *English Gothic: Classic Horror Cinema*. London: Signum Books, 2015.

Simpson, M. J. *Urban Terrors: New British Horror Cinema, 1997–2008*. Bristol, UK: Hemlock Books, 2012.

Walker, Johnny. *Contemporary British Horror Cinema: Industry, Genre and Society*. Edinburgh: Edinburgh UP, 2016.

Worland, Rick. *The Horror Film: An Introduction*. Oxford, UK: Blackwell, 2007.

WORKS CITED

Alexander, Dave. "*Outpost*." *Rue Morgue* 78 (May 2008).

Bawdon, Fiona. "Hoodie or Altar Boys?" Women in Journalism 10 Mar. 2009. www.womeninjournalism.co.uk.

Bennett, Ray. "*Severance* Film Review." *Hollywood Reporter* 13 Sept. 2006. Accessed 1 Sept. 2016, www.movie-film -review.com.

Biancolli, Ann. "*The Woman in Black* Review: Radcliff Goes Gothic." *San Francisco Chronicle* 3 Feb. 2012.

Bitel, Anton. "*F*." *Little White Lies*. 23 Sept. 2010.

———. "*Outpost*." *Eye for Film* 15 May 2008. www.eyeforfilm .co.uk.

Bradshaw, Peter. "*Eden Lake* Film Review." *Guardian* 12 Sept. 2008.

———. "*F*." Film review. *Guardian* 16 Sept. 2010.

Cameron, David. "To Fix Broken Britain We Will Start at School." *Telegraph* 2 Sept. 2007.

Clarens, Carlos. *An Illustrated History of Horror and Science-Fiction Films*. 1967. Reprint, London: Da Capo, 1997.

Clarke, Donald. "Subterranean Sick Blues." *Irish Times* 9 July 2005.

Clover, Carol. *Men, Women and Chainsaws: Gender in the Modern Horror Film*. Princeton, NJ: Princeton UP, 1992.

Collin, Robbie. "*The Woman in Black* Review." *Telegraph* 9 Feb. 2012.

Collins, David. "Family Valu£s: The People Looks at Controversial Bid to Tame Young Thugs." *People* 1 June 2008.

Cooper, David. *The Death of the Family*. London: Allen Lane, 1971.

"*The Descent* Film Review." *Total Film* 10 Oct. 2012.

Duncan, Lizzie. "*F.*" Film review. *HorrorNews.net* 25 Oct. 2015.

Ebert, Roger. "*The Descent*." *RogerEbert.com* 3 Aug. 2006.

———. "*The Woman in Black*." *RogerEbert.com* 1 Feb. 2012.

Elley, Derek. "*Severance* Film Review." *Variety* 16 Sept. 2006. Accessed 1 Sept. 2016, www.movie-film-review.com.

———. "*Triangle*: Film Review." *Variety* 8 Nov. 2009.

Evans, Tim. "*Severance* Film Review." *Sky Movies*. Accessed 1 Sept. 2016, www.movie-film-review.com.

Felperin, Leslie. "*Mum and Dad*." *Variety* 30 June 2008.

Floyd, Nigel. "*Triangle*: Film Review." *Time Out* 15 Oct. 2009.

Forshaw, Barry. *British Gothic Cinema*. Basingstoke, UK: Palgrave Macmillan, 2013.

Frank, Alan G. *Horror Movies*. London: Octopus, 1974.

French, Philip. "*Outpost*: Review." *Observer* 18 May 2008.

———. "*Severance* Film Review." *Guardian* 27 Aug. 2006.

———. "*Triangle*: Film Review." *Observer* 18 Oct. 2009.

Gant, Charles. "*F*: Film Review." *Variety* 20 Sept. 2010.

Garner, Richard. "'Hoodies, Louts, Scum': How Media Demonises Teenagers; Research Finds Negative Stories in the Press Make Teenage Boys Frightened of Each Other." *Independent* 13 Mar. 2009.

Gifford, Dennis. *A Pictorial History of the Horror Movies.* London: Hamlyn, 1973.

Goldstein, Gary. "Movie Review: *Heartless.*" *Los Angeles Times* 1 June 2010.

Gore, Lucius. "*Triangle*: Film Review." *ESplatter* 20 Feb. 2010. www.ESplatter.com.

Graham, Jane. "Hoodies Strike Fear in British Cinema." *Guardian* 5 Nov. 2009.

Grantham. Scott. "*Lighthouse*: A Review." *Video Watchdog* July 2000.

Hardy, Phil. *The Encyclopedia of Horror Movies.* London: HarperCollins, 1986.

Harvey, Denis. "Review: *Eden Lake.*" *Variety* 3 Nov. 2008.

Heilman, Jeremy. "*Outpost.*" *MovieMartyr* 7 July 2008. www .moviemartyr.com.

Hess, Alex. "*Eden Lake*: The Film That Frightened Me Most." *Guardian* 11 Sept. 2008. www.guardian.com.

Higson, Andrew. *Dissolving Views: Key Writings on British Cinema.* London: Wellington House, 1996.

Hills, Matt. "Hammer 2.0: Legacy, Modernization, and Hammer Horror as Heritage Brand." *Merchants of Menace: The Business of Horror Cinema.* Ed. Richard Nowell. London: Bloomsbury, 2014. 229–49.

Holden, Stephen. "*Lighthouse*: So Where's Virginia Woolf When You Need Her?" *New York Times* 4 Feb. 2000.

Hutchings, Peter. "London Horror." *Journal of British Cinema and Television* 6.2 (2009): 190–206.

———. "Uncanny Landscapes in British Film and Television." *Visual Culture in Britain* 5.2 (2004): 27–40.

Jollin, Dan. "*The Descent*: Review." *Empire* July 2005.

Kraceur, Siegfried. *From Caligari to Hitler*. 1947. Princeton, NJ: Princeton UP, 2004.

Leggott, James. *Contemporary British Cinema: From Heritage to Horror*. London: Wallflower, 2008.

Lilleyman, Sarah. "A Genuinely Creepy *Descent*." *Time* 5 Aug. 2006.

Macdonald, Scott. "*Outpost*." *Eye for Film* 21 June 2008. www.eyeforfilm.co.uk.

Meikle, Dennis. *A History of Horrors: The Rise and Fall of the House of Hammer*. Rev. ed. Lanham, MD: Scarecrow, 2009.

Moore, Debi. "*Severance*." *Dread Central* 1 Apr. 2007. www.dreadcentral.com.

Murray, James, Dave Robbers, and Matt Drake. "Should Hooded Youths Be Banned from Our Streets and Shops?" *Sunday Express* 30 Mar. 2008.

Newman, Kim. "*Lighthouse* Review." *Empire* July 2000.

Nusair, David. "*Outpost*." *Reel Film Reviews* 13 May 2008. www.reelfilm.com.

Pirie, David. *A Heritage of Horror: The Gothic English Cinema 1946–1972*. London: Gordon Fraser, 1973.

Pvt.Caboose91. "*Outpost*." *Manly Movie* 24 Feb. 2015. www.manlymovie.net.

Rawson-Jones, Ben. "*Heartless*." *Digital Spy* 19 May 2010. www.digitalspy.com.

Rigby, Jonathan. *English Gothic: A Century of Horror Cinema*. London: Reynolds and Hearn, 2006.

Sean and Monkeyface. "*Severance*." *Internal Bleeding* Aug. 2008. www.internalbleeding.net.

Shail, Robert. *The Children's Film Foundation*. London: BFI, 2016.

Simpson, M. J. *Urban Terrors: New British Horror Cinema 1997–2008*. Bristol, UK: Hemlock Books, 2012.

Smith, Kyle. "Heartless." *New York Post* 19 Nov. 2010.

Stanley, Richard. "Dying Light: An Obituary for the Great British Horror Movie." *British Horror Cinema*. Ed. S. Chibnall and J. Petley. London: Routledge, 2002. 183–95.

Thomas, William. "*Triangle*: Film Review." *Empire* 1 Oct. 2009.

Thurman, Trace. "10 Must-See Independent Horror Films of 2016." *Bloody Disgusting* 20 Jan. 2016. http://bloody-disgusting.com.

Tookey, Christopher. "*Eden Lake*: A Great Movie (If You Can Stomach It)." *Daily Mail* 11 Sept. 2008.

Toy, Sam. "*Severance*." *Empire* 29 July 2006.

Travers, Peter. "*Severance* Film Review." *Rolling Stone* 18 Apr. 2007.

Turner, Matthew. "*Mum and Dad*." *View London Review* 22 Dec. 2008.

Tyler, Imogen. *Revolting Subjects: Social Abjection and Resistance in Neoliberal Britain*. London: Zed Books, 2013.

"Under That Hoodie Is a Child like Yours." *Daily Mail* 15 May 2005.

Vasquez, Felix, Jr. "*F*." Film review. *Cinema Crazed* 10 Sept. 2016. www.cinema-crazed.com.

Walker, Johnny. *Contemporary British Horror Cinema: Industry, Genre and Society*. Edinburgh: Edinburgh UP, 2016.

Wright, Tristan. "*Outpost*." *Movies Made Me* 21 Apr. 2009. www.moviesmademe.com.

MAGAZINES, FILMS, TV SERIES

MAGAZINES

Diabolique (2010–present)
Famous Monsters of Filmland (1958–present)
Fangoria (1979)
House of Hammer (1976–78)
Monster Mag (1974–76)
Monster Mania (1966–67)
Rue Morgue (1997–present)
We Belong Dead (1993–present)

FILMS

Note: Some of these films are coproductions between the UK and other countries. For sake of brevity, details regarding exact countries of origin have not been included.

The Abandoned (Nacho Cerda, 2006)
ABCs of Death (various directors, 2012)
Anazapta (Alberto Sciamma, 2002)
Attack the Block (Joe Cornish, 2011)
The Awakening (Nick Murphy, 2011)
Berberian Sound Studio (Peter Strickland, 2012)
Beyond the Rave (Matthias Hoene, 2008)

Black Death (Christopher Smith, 2010)

The Borderlands (Elliot Goldner, 2013)

Botched (Kit Ryan, 2008)

Boy Eats Girl (Stephen Bradley, 2005)

The Broken (Sean Ellis, 2008)

The Bunker (Rob Green, 2002)

Byzantium (Neil Jordan, 2012)

Cherry Tree Lane (Paul Andrew Williams, 2010)

The Children (Tom Shankland, 2008)

Citadel (Ciaran Foy, 2012)

Cockneys versus Zombies (Matthias Hoene, 2012)

Colin (Marc Price, 2008)

Comedown (Menhaj Huda, 2012)

Community (Jason Ford, 2012)

The Cottage (Paul Andrew Williams, 2008)

Creep (Christopher Smith, 2004)

The Dark (John Fawcett, 2005)

Dark Night (Daniel Grant, 2006)

The Dead (Howard Ford and Jon Ford, 2010)

Dead Man's Shoes (Shane Meadows, 2004)

Death Walks (Spencer Hawken, 2016)

Deathwatch (Michael J. Bassett, 2002)

Definition of Fear (James Simpson, 2017)

The Descent (Neil Marshall, 2005)

The Descent, Part 2 (Jon Harris, 2009)

Devil's Business (Sean Hogan, 2011)

The Disappeared (Johnny Kevorkian, 2008)

Dog Soldiers (Neil Marshall, 2002)

Doghouse (Jake West, 2009)

Doomsday (Neil Marshall, 2008)

Dorian Gray (Oliver Parker, 2009)

Eden Lake (James Watkins, 2008)

Evil Aliens (Jake West, 2005)

The Evolved (Andrew Senior and John Turner, 2006)

F (Johannes Roberts, 2010)

For Those in Peril (Paul Wright, 2013)

The Forest (Jason Zada, 2016)

The Girl with All the Gifts (Colm McCarthy, 2016)

Grabbers (Jon Wright, 2012)

Heartless (Philip Ridley, 2009)

The Hole (Nick Hamm, 2001)

Howl (Paul Hyett, 2015)

Hush (Mark Tonderai, 2008)

Inbred (Alex Chandon, 2011)

Kill List (Ben Wheatley, 2011)

The Last Great Wilderness (David Mackenzie, 2003)

The Last Horror Movie (Julian Richards, 2003)

Lesbian Vampire Killers (Phil Claydon, 2009)

Let Me In (Matt Reeves, 2010)

Lighthouse (Simon Hunter, 2000)

London Voodoo (Robert Pratten, 2004)

A Lonely Place to Die (Julian Gilbey, 2011)

Monsters (Gareth Edwards, 2010)

Mum & Dad (Steven Sheil, 2008)

My Little Eye (Marc Evans, 2002)

Nina Forever (Ben Blaine and Chris Blaine, 2015)

Outpost (Steve Barker, 2008)

Outpost II: Black Sun (Steve Barker, 2012)

Outpost III: Rise of the Spetsnaz (Kieran Parker, 2013)

Pride, Prejudice and Zombies (Burr Steers, 2016)

Psychosis (Reg Travista, 2010)
Puffball (Nicolas Roeg, 2007)
The Quiet Ones (John Pogue, 2014)
The Reeds (Nick Cohen, 2010)
The Resident (Antti Jokinen, 2010)
Resident Evil (Paul W. S. Anderson, 2002)
Salvage (Lawrence Gough, 2009)
Sawney: Flesh of Man (Ricky Wood, 2013)
Scrawl (Peter Hearn, 2015)
The Seasoning House (Paul Hyatt, 2012)
Severance (Christopher Smith, 2006)
Shaun of the Dead (Edgar Wright, 2004)
Sightseers (Ben Wheatley, 2012)
Soulmate (Axelle Carolyn, 2013)
Stitches (Connor McMahon, 2012)
Stoker (Park Chan-Wook, 2013)
Strange Factories (John Harrigan, 2013)
Strangers Within (Liam Hooper, 2015)
Tony (Gerard Johnson, 2009)
Tower Block (James Nunn and Ronnie Thompson, 2012)
Triangle (Christopher Smith, 2009)
28 Days Later (Danny Boyle, 2002)
28 Weeks Later (Juan Carlos Fresnadillo, 2007)
Under the Skin (Jonathan Glazer, 2013)
The Unkindness of Ravens (Lawrie Brewster, 2016)
Wake Wood (David Keating, 2009)
When the Lights Went Out (Pat Holden, 2012)
White Settlers (Simeon Halligan, 2014)
Wilderness (Michael J. Bassett, 2006)
The Woman in Black (James Watkins, 2012)

The Woman in Black: The Angel of Death (Tom Harper, 2015)
The World's End (Edgar Wright, 2013)
WΔZ (Tom Shankland, 2007)

TV SERIES

Being Human (UK, 2009–13)
A Ghost Story for Christmas (UK, 1971–78)
Ghostwatch (UK, 1992)
Hi de Hi! (UK, 1980–88)
Home and Away (Australia, 1988–present)
Most Haunted (UK, 2002–present)
Oh, Doctor Beeching! (UK, 1995–97)
Sea of Souls (UK, 2004–7)
Spaced (UK, 1999–2001)
The Stone Tape (UK, 1972)
You Rang, M'Lord? (UK, 1988–93)

INDEX

ABOUT THE AUTHOR

Steven Gerrard is a senior lecturer at the Northern Film School, Leeds Beckett University. He also lectures at the University of Wales. His monograph *The Carry On Films* celebrates those bastions of all things naughty but nice, and he has published extensively for *We Belong Dead*, *Dark Side,* and others. In his spare time, he longs to be either the new Doctor Who or Status Quo's rhythm guitarist. He'll have a long wait.